EAT DES

PROFIT, POWER, AND THE END OF POVERTY RULES IN A MILLION-DOLLAR FIRM

T. JAYDEN DOYÉ, CPA

For more information, email jayden@prestigeaccountants.com.

Disclaimer

The information contained in this book, **Eat Dessert First**, is provided for **educational and informational purposes only**. It is not intended as, and should not be construed as, legal, tax, accounting, financial, or mental health advice.

While the author, **Jayden Doyé, CPA**, draws on professional experience working with law firm owners, **no professional relationship is created** between you and the author, the publisher, or Prestige Accounting & Consulting by your reading this book. This book does not create a CPA–client relationship, an attorney–client relationship, or any other professional advisory relationship.

You should not act or refrain from acting based on any content included in this book without seeking appropriate, individualized advice from a licensed attorney, certified public accountant, tax professional, financial advisor, therapist, or other qualified professional in your jurisdiction. Your situation is unique, and the strategies or examples in this book may not be appropriate for your specific circumstances.

All examples, case studies, and characters referenced in this book are **hypothetical, composite, or anonymized** and are used for illustrative purposes only. Any resemblance to actual persons, living or dead, or to actual firms or cases, is coincidental and unintentional.

Every effort has been made to ensure the accuracy of the information presented at the time of publication; however, laws, regulations, financial standards, and best practices **change over**

time. The author and publisher make **no representations or warranties**, express or implied, about the completeness, accuracy, reliability, suitability, or availability of the information contained herein.

Any income figures, revenue milestones, profit margins, or growth outcomes discussed in this book are **illustrative only**. There is **no guarantee** that you or your law firm will achieve the same or similar results. Your results will depend on a variety of factors, including but not limited to your market, practice area, team, systems, effort, and decision-making.

By reading this book, you acknowledge and agree that the author and publisher are **not responsible or liable** for any loss, damage, or adverse consequences that may arise from your use of, or reliance on, the information contained herein. You accept full responsibility for your own decisions, actions, and results, and you agree to consult qualified professionals before implementing any strategy discussed in this book.

If you need legal, tax, accounting, financial planning, or mental health services, you should contact a licensed professional in your area.

TABLE OF CONTENTS

Introduction

Have you ever felt like your law firm is thriving while you're left scraping by on the crumbs? As lawyers, you've been indoctrinated with an unspoken hierarchy that goes something like this: serve the clients, pay the staff, cover the bills, and only then see if there's anything left for us. It sounds noble, right? On paper, it feels responsible and even sacrificial. In reality, it's a surefire recipe for resentment, burnout, and those late-night Google searches for "non-legal careers that pay well."

I see it too often among law firm owners across the country. They're pulling in impressive revenues—$800,000, $1.2 million, even $2 million—but what do they actually take home? It often resembles a decent paralegal's salary. Stress levels? Sky-high. Picture this: One email away from breaking down in the bathroom, wondering how you can run a million-dollar business yet feel so financially depleted.

This is where the problem lies. Many of us grew up in environments where money was tight, where the belief was that as long as the bills were paid, things were fine. Now, as firm owners, you've upgraded the bills, yet the same scarcity mindset lingers. Your firm is feasting on steak and lobster while you've got cereal in your pantry. So let's flip the script.

Welcome to the "Eat Dessert First" philosophy. This book is designed to challenge everything you've been taught about your financial worth as a lawyer. Traditionally, dessert was a rare treat, something you earned only when others were satisfied. Many law firm owners treat their profits and well-being with the same caution: "If there's enough left over," "If I'm not too busy," or "Maybe next month." But that approach doesn't lead to a First-Class Firm.

In these pages, we'll explore how to build your firm intentionally, prioritizing your profit, taxes, pay, and mental health from the start. By embracing the philosophy of "eating dessert first," you're making a declaration: "I am no longer willing to be the least taken care of person in my own business."

I invite you to join me on a journey where you step into your power as a firm owner. Together, we will tackle the barriers that keep you from scaling your firm while keeping you stuck in survival mode. Whether you're a seasoned owner or just starting, this book aims to transform your mindset and your business.

So why should you read on? It's time to redefine what success looks like for you, shift from survival to strategic growth, and finally take control of your financial narrative. Let's embark on this journey to discover how you can build a First-Class Firm that honors your worth, respects your sacrifices, and ultimately serves you. It all starts here—deciding that you deserve dessert, and together, we'll climb to new heights.

CHAPTER 1

Eat Dessert First: Why Your Law Firm Is Eating Better Than You

Let me start with something a little uncomfortable:

There are way too many law firm owners out here running **seven-figure firms**… while personally living on emotional and financial crumbs.

Your staff is eating.

Your vendors are eating.

Your landlord stays full.

Even your case management software is on direct debit, living its best life.

Meanwhile, you—the one who actually took the bar exam, the one who took on all the risk—are over here trying to figure out why your bank account doesn't match your Instagram.

If that stung a little, good. You're in the right book.

When the Firm Eats First

Most lawyers were trained to think like this:

- Serve the clients
- Pay the staff
- Cover all the bills
- *Then* see what's left over for you

On paper, that sounds noble. Responsible. Sacrificial even.

In real life?

It's the fastest way to resent your firm, burn out, and secretly Google "non-legal careers that pay well" at 2 a.m.

I work with law firm owners all over the country, and I see the same pattern over and over again:

- Revenue: $800,000, $1.2M, $2M+
- Owner's actual take-home: looks like a decent paralegal's salary
- Stress level: one email away from crying in the bathroom

And here's the wild part—many of these owners **grew up like I did**: in or near poverty, where money was always tight, and you were taught things like:

"As long as the bills are paid, we're okay."

So now, as a firm owner, you've upgraded the bills—but kept the same mindset.

Your firm is eating steak and lobster.

You're looking at your account like, *"How do I have a million-dollar business and still feel broke?"*

Let's fix that.

The Eat Dessert First Philosophy

This book is called **Eat Dessert First** for a reason.

Growing up, dessert was rare. You didn't just get dessert because you felt like it. You got dessert if:

- The lights stayed on
- Nobody cussed at the mailbox when the bills came
- And your parent or guardian was in a good enough mood

Dessert was a privilege, not a plan.

Most law firm owners treat **profit** and **their own well-being** the same way.

"If there's enough left over…"

"If we have a good month…"

"If I'm not too busy putting out fires…"

Then you'll think about yourself. Maybe.

But a First-Class Firm doesn't work like that.

A First-Class Firm is built on **intentionality**—with your profit, your taxes, your pay, and your mental health.

So here's the core philosophy of this book:

You don't create a successful firm and *then* decide to eat dessert.

You decide to eat dessert first, and then you build the firm around that decision.

That's not selfish. That's strategy.

That's you saying, "I will not recreate poverty rules in a million-dollar business."

Your Bank Accounts as Food Groups

Because I'm a foodie, and because metaphors make money easier to talk about, we're going to think about your firm's bank accounts as **food groups**.

Most law firm owners treat their operating account like one **giant pot of gumbo**. Everything just gets thrown in:

- Retainers
- Settlements
- Fees
- Refunds
- Payroll
- Subscriptions
- Random Amazon orders that *"we needed for the office."*

And then you look at the pot and guess how much you can afford.

That's not a system.

That's vibes.

So instead of one big pot, I want you to imagine four separate plates:

1. **Dessert – Profit (at least 5%)**

2. **Carbs – Tax Savings (around 10%)**
3. **Vegetables – Owner Benefits (aiming for 30%+)**
4. **Meat – Operating Expenses (everything else)**

Let's break these down.

Dessert – Profit (Minimum 5%): The First Bite

Let's be clear: dessert is not the leftover crumbs after everybody else eats.

Dessert is the part you **set aside first on purpose**, even when it feels uncomfortable.

In money terms, dessert is your **profit—your reward for owning the firm**, not working in it.

And I'm talking about real profit. Not "Well, technically, after I do this twelve-tab spreadsheet and add back this and subtract that, there's a profit."

No. I mean, **cash** that gets set aside and is not for payroll, not for rent, not for paying AmEx because you went on a software shopping spree.

Why start with 5%?

Because almost every firm—even the messy, stressed-out ones—can carve out **five cents of every dollar** and not die.

Will it feel tight? Yes.

Will it expose waste? Absolutely.

Will it force you to stop pretending the firm is a bottomless ATM? 100%.

But more importantly, **it will start re-wiring your brain.**

See, when you grow up in scarcity, your nervous system gets used to:

- Waiting for the other shoe to drop
- Expecting emergencies
- Believing you're "being greedy" if you want more than "just enough."

So even when you have more money, you still operate as if it could vanish at any moment.

Setting aside profit *first* is about more than numbers.

It says to your nervous system:

"We are no longer in survival mode. We are building something stable."

That little 5% is dessert, yes—but it's also **evidence**.

Evidence that you can create a margin.

Evidence that you deserve more than struggle.

Carbs – Tax Savings (10%): Protect Your Peace from the IRS

Let's talk about the food most of us secretly love but pretend we're above: **carbs**.

Your **Carbs Account** is your **tax savings account**.

Now listen… the IRS does not care about your feelings. They do not care that your staff is expensive, that Meta ads are high, or that your landlord just went up on rent.

They want their cut.

Yet every year, I see law firm owners acting surprised at tax time, as if the government just invented taxes last Tuesday.

Tax stress is not just a money issue. It's a **mental health issue**.

That anxiety you feel in your chest every time your CPA emails you? That's your nervous system remembering years of "I owe how much!?"

When we don't intentionally set money aside for taxes:

- We avoid looking at reports
- We procrastinate on filing
- We make short-term, panic-driven decisions
- We underpay ourselves because "What if I need it for taxes?"

In this framework, **10% of your gross revenue** is deposited into your Carbs Account.

Not at the end of the year.

Not "when things calm down."

Every single time money comes in.

This isn't just smart. It's **self-care**.

You are giving Future You a gift: the gift of not having a panic attack on the phone with your tax preparer. You are reducing stress, and that matters because an anxious brain does not make million-dollar decisions.

Vegetables – Owner Benefits (30%+): Feeding the Person Who Built the Firm

Let's be honest. Growing up, a lot of us had a complicated relationship with vegetables.

We were told:

"Eat your vegetables so you can grow."

"Eat what's on your plate; there are starving children somewhere."

So you choke down the veggies because someone else said it was "good for you," not because you actually felt nourished.

As a law firm owner, **you are the vegetable**.

You are the thing that must be healthy for the rest of the plate to make sense.

Your **Vegetable Account** is where we make sure **you** are getting at least **30% of the business's economic benefit**, through a mix of:

- Salary
- Owner's distributions
- Business-paid benefits and perks that are legally and ethically structured

For many of you, this is where the mindset war shows up.

Here are some of the things I hear all the time:

- "I'll pay myself more once we hit [insert arbitrary revenue number]."

- "It feels selfish to take more when I could hire another person."
- "My staff has families to feed."
- "I don't really *need* more right now."

And I get it. You care about your team. You care about your clients.

But here's the truth:

When the owner is depleted, everybody eventually pays for it.

Depleted owners:

- Snap at staff
- Stay stuck working in the weeds because they can't afford help
- Make desperate marketing decisions
- Say yes to bad-fit clients because they "need the money."
- Secretly consider closing down what could be a thriving firm

Making sure you are fed is not about greed; it's about **stability**.

You are the leader. Leaders need rest, margin, therapy, vacations, and sometimes that soft life moment on a beach with a drink that has too many syllables.

That doesn't happen by accident.

It happens when we *plan* for you to receive at least 30%.

Meat – Operating Expenses: Everything Else Gets What's Left

Finally, we've got the **Meat Account**—your **operating expenses**.

Most law firms operate like the meat is the main character. The firm eats first:

- Fancy office lease
- All the subscriptions
- Staff before the firm is structurally ready
- Sponsoring every event because of "exposure."

And then you look at what's left and hope it's enough for dessert, carbs, and veggies.

We're flipping that.

In this model, **meat gets what's left** after:

- Profit is set aside
- Taxes are covered
- The owner is cared for

Now, I already know what somebody is thinking:

"If I did that, my firm couldn't afford what we're paying right now."

And I'm telling you, as lovingly as I can:

Exactly.

The point is not to make money appear magically.

The point is to tell the truth about what your firm can support *without* sacrificing your mental health and your long-term wealth.

Tightening up the meat category forces you to ask:

- Do we really need this?
- Are we getting a return on this expense?
- Is there a more efficient way?
- Are we hiding poor boundaries and poor leadership behind "I'll just throw money at it"?

Constraints are not punishment.

Constraints are how you build **a firm that lasts.**

Meet Monique: A Million-Dollar Firm and a Broke CEO

Let me introduce you to **Monique Johnson, Esq.**

She's not a real, single person—but she's very real. She's a composite of so many lawyers I've worked with.

Monique owns a small but mighty **family law firm** in a major city.

On paper, she's killing it:

- $1.1 million in annual revenue
- Team of five: two associates, a paralegal, an assistant, and an intake coordinator
- Beautiful office with exposed brick and good lighting for reels
- Followers on social who see her as *the* go-to attorney for high-conflict divorces

But here's what you don't see on Instagram:

- She hasn't paid herself a consistent salary in six months.
- Every tax season, she ends up on a payment plan… again.
- She wakes up at 3 a.m. thinking about payroll.
- She's drinking way too much coffee, not enough water, and her therapist keeps asking, "So when are you going to slow down?"

Monique came to me saying, "I think we have a cash flow problem."

But what she really had was a **mindset problem**, wrapped in a **systems problem**, seasoned with a **little bit of financial chaos**.

Money came into one main operating account. Everything got paid from that account: staff, rent, taxes, her personal bills when she was short, random business expenses, and impulsive marketing.

There was no plan—just vibes and invoices.

When we looked at the numbers for the previous year, here's what we saw:

- Revenue: Just over $1.1M
- Net profit: Technically small, but on a cash basis, she was constantly strapped
- Owner's true economic benefit: maybe 12–15% when we added salary + distributions + benefits

Twelve to fifteen percent… on a million-dollar firm.

You don't need a CPA to tell you that the math does not match the sacrifice.

On top of that, the emotional cost was high. She was exhausted, snapping at her kids, and seriously considering going back to being someone else's employee "just for a while."

That's what happens when the firm eats better than you.

The Mindset Behind the Mess

When we dug deeper, Monique's money story started to sound familiar:

- She grew up in a single-parent home where money was always tight.
- Her mother would say things like, "As long as the bills are paid, we're okay."
- She was the "smart one" in the family, so she felt responsible for "making it" and helping everyone else.

So now, as a law firm owner:

- She paid staff first, even when numbers were shaky.
- She'd rather be stressed out personally than lay someone off.
- She felt guilty about increasing her own salary.
- She over-delivered for low-paying clients because "they really need help."

Here's the problem with that:

Poverty rules do not work in a million-dollar business.

You can't build a First-Class Firm while following survival-mode rules.

Survival-mode says:

- "I'll be okay as long as everybody else is okay."
- "I'm strong. I can take it."
- "I don't want to seem greedy."

First-Class Firm mindset says:

- "Everyone will be okay because I am stable… and I refuse to lead from lack."

The turning point for Monique wasn't me giving her a fancy spreadsheet.

It was this moment, when I asked her:

"Do you realize you've built a million-dollar firm that treats you like you're still the little girl hoping the lights stay on?"

She paused.

She cried.

Then she laughed through tears and said, "You didn't have to read me like that."

That's the power of bringing **mindset and psychology** into money conversations.

Until you acknowledge the emotional script running in the background, every new strategy will eventually get dragged back down to the level of your old beliefs.

Implementing the Food Group System (Without Losing Your Mind)

We didn't flip a switch and fix everything overnight. This isn't a Netflix makeover show.

Here's what we did with Monique, step-by-step:

1. **We set a small, non-negotiable dessert portion.** We started with **5% of every dollar** going into a separate profit account. No exceptions. Even when she complained. Even when it felt tight.
2. **We opened a separate Carbs (Tax) account.** Each week, 10% of the collected revenue is moved into that account. That money was off-limits for day-to-day drama.
3. **We defined a realistic vegetable goal.** Based on her revenue, we set a target for her to receive at least **30% of her total** compensation (salary, distributions, and legitimate benefits). She wasn't there yet, but we had a **destination**.
4. **We forced the meat category to fit what remained.** That meant tough choices:
    - Cutting subscriptions that no one was using
    - Renegotiating vendor contracts
    - Letting go of one underperforming role
    - Saying no to certain sponsorships and "look good" expenses

Was it uncomfortable? Absolutely.

But within months:

- Her tax anxiety dropped dramatically.

- She was paying herself consistently.
- There was actual profit sitting in an account in her name.
- Her brain went from constantly bracing for disaster to finally exhaling.

And that mental shift?

That's what gave her the capacity to think clearly about **scaling** instead of just **surviving**.

The Psychology of Scaling: Why Strategy Isn't Enough

Here's something you need to understand if you're anywhere near that million-dollar mark:

The biggest barrier to scaling is rarely strategy. Its identity.

You can implement all the food-group accounts, all the KPIs, all the dashboards.

But if you still see yourself as:

- The broke kid who should just be grateful
- The savior who must struggle for everyone else to be okay
- The hustler who only feels valuable when exhausted

...then you will unconsciously make decisions that drag you back to that familiar struggle.

Scaling a firm requires you to become someone who:

- Believes it's safe to have money

- Believes it's safe to rest
- Believes it's safe to say no
- Believes it's safe to let the business be bigger than your trauma

That's not fluffy mindset talk. That's **operational reality**.

Because a regulated, well-rested, well-paid CEO:

- Delegates better
- Hires more intentionally
- Takes smarter risks
- Knows when to walk away from bad-fit clients
- Builds systems instead of constantly firefighting

Whereas an exhausted, underpaid, anxious CEO will always end up:

- Overworking
- People-pleasing
- Hoarding control
- Sabotaging growth opportunities

In other words:

Your nervous system is either your silent business partner or your silent saboteur.

Dessert First Is Self-Respect

This is why we start the entire book here—with dessert.

Not because I want you to go wild and buy a new car tomorrow.

But because I want you to build a firm that:

- Respects your sacrifice
- Honors your story
- Protects your mental health
- Funds your actual life, not just your office life

When you decide to **eat dessert first**, you are making a declaration:

"I am no longer willing to be the least taken care of person in my own business."

You are saying:

- I matter.
- My mental health matters.
- My rest matters.
- My wealth matters.

And from that place, you can make clear, strategic decisions that will truly scale your firm.

A First-Class Firm is not just about the number on your P&L.

It's about the quality of life of the person who owns it.

Your First Action Step

Before we move to the next chapter, I want you to do one simple, powerful thing.

Not a spreadsheet. Not a forecast. Just this:

Look at your last 12 months and answer these questions honestly:

1. Roughly what percentage of your revenue actually ended up in your pocket—salary, distributions, perks, and all?
2. How much of your stress in the last year was directly tied to money—payroll, taxes, or your own personal bills?
3. If your firm were a dinner plate, which one is getting the biggest serving right now: dessert, carbs, veggies, or meat?

No judgment. No shame. Just data.

Because in the chapters ahead, I'm going to show you how to use the **C.L.I.M.B. Methodology** to transform your firm into a First-Class Firm.

But it all starts right here:

With you deciding that you deserve dessert,

And you're done building businesses that starve you.

Let's climb.

CHAPTER 2

Vegetables First: Why Your Owner's Pay Is Non-Negotiable

Let's start with a hard truth:

If your firm is making close to or over a million dollars and you're still scared to open your personal banking app… something is broken.

Not "Oh, I just need a better marketing funnel" broken.

I mean, *spiritually* broken. The nervous system is broken. "How did I work this hard and still feel broke?" broken.

You did not go to law school, pass the bar, build a whole firm, and employ other grown people to end up **last in line** for your own money.

We're not doing that anymore.

When the Boss Is the Brokest Person in the Building

In Chapter 1, we talked about your money as food groups:

- **Dessert** – Profit
- **Carbs** – Tax Savings

- **Vegetables** – Owner Benefits
- **Meat** – Operating Expenses

This chapter is all about the **vegetables**—you.

Now, I know vegetables don't sound sexy.

As kids, a lot of us were told, "Eat your vegetables so you can grow," while adults hovered over us like we were in a hostage situation with green beans.

So now, you're a law firm owner doing the same thing to yourself:

You're forcing yourself to swallow whatever's left of life and money after everybody else is fed, hoping **that** will somehow help you "grow."

But here's the reality:

Your firm cannot be a First-Class Firm if the person flying the plane is malnourished.

The owner's pay is not "whatever is left."

Owner's pay is **a line item, a decision, and a boundary.**

What "Owner Benefits" Really Mean

When I say **owner benefits**, I'm not just talking about a paycheck.

I'm talking about the **total economic benefit** you receive from your firm:

- Your **salary** (the consistent, predictable part)

- Your **owner's distributions** (extra cash you pull out as the firm performs)
- Legitimate **business-paid expenses** that improve your life and are correctly structured from a tax and compliance standpoint

Altogether, my goal for you is to ensure that **at least 30%** of your firm's economic value flows to you.

Why?

Because a First-Class Firm isn't just defined by revenue. The baseline picture we're building toward is:

- $1M+ in annual revenue
- $100k+ in true profit
- $100k+ in owner's compensation

You are not just an employee of your business. You're the founder, the risk taker, the one who signed for the lease and sat through those client meetings that should've come with hazard pay.

You deserve more than "whatever is left."

How Poverty Rules Sneak Into Your Paycheck

Let's be real for a second.

A lot of law firm owners grew up on some version of:

- "As long as the bills are paid, we're okay."
- "We don't talk about money in this house."
- "Be grateful. Other people have it worse."

So now, you're grown with a whole firm, and that same script is still running:

- "As long as payroll is made, I'm okay."
- "I don't *need* to pay myself more."
- "I'll take care of myself once the firm is more stable."

That sounds humble. It even sounds noble.

But it's really just **survival mode with a nicer office.**

When you underpay yourself, here's what actually happens:

- You **personally feel stressed**, so you cling to control rather than delegating.
- You say yes to **bad-fit clients** because you're scared to lose money.
- You overwork because "I can't afford to take time off."
- You start to quietly resent the very business you built.

That's not leadership. That's martyrdom in a blazer.

Monique's Wake-Up Call

Let's go back to **Monique**, our family law attorney from Chapter 1.

Once we implemented the food group accounts and got her dessert (profit) and carbs (tax) flowing, we turned to her vegetables.

When we calculated her **true owner benefit** for the prior year—salary, distributions, and perks—it came out to about **14%** of revenue.

Fourteen.

On a firm bringing in over a million.

When I told her the number, she stared for a second, laughed, and said, "So you're telling me my firm eats like it's at Ruth's Chris and I'm at home making struggle spaghetti?"

Exactly.

And just like a lot of you, she had a **reason** for everything:

- "I wanted to hire more help for the team."
- "The office needed to look nice for the type of clients we serve."
- "I didn't want my staff to worry about their checks."

All beautiful intentions.

All rooted in something dangerous:

"Everyone else deserves stability more than I do."

Once we named it, she realized something:

She had recreated the emotional dynamics of her childhood—where her job was to be "responsible" for everyone else—inside her firm.

Same script. Bigger numbers.

That's when the shift started.

Designing Non-Negotiable Owner Pay

We didn't jump straight from 14% to 30%. This is not a TikTok before-and-after.

Here's how we approached it—step by step:

1. We Defined the Target

First, we ran some quick numbers:

At $1.1M in revenue, a **30% owner benefit** target meant about **$330,000** in total compensation per year.

That could look like:

- A base salary of $180–200k
- Plus $130–150k in distributions and business-paid benefits over the year

We wrote that down. Not as a fantasy. As a **target**.

2. We Set a Floor, Not Just a Ceiling

Then we set a **minimum owner's salary** she would get every month, no matter what.

No more "let me see what's left after everyone else."

Her pay became a **fixed part of the budget**, just like rent.

That alone changed the energy. She was no longer hoping to pay herself. She was committing to it.

3. We Created a Path to 30%

We looked at:

- Where expenses could be trimmed
- Where pricing needed to increase
- Where low-value work could be cut or delegated

Every improvement freed up capacity to move her closer to that 30% goal.

We celebrated every step—18%, 21%, 24%—because each shift wasn't just more money. It was **evidence** that she was no longer willing to be last in line.

What Happens When the Owner Finally Gets Fed

Here's what surprised Monique the most:

As her compensation increased, her **anxiety decreased**... and her leadership got better.

With consistent, fair pay:

- She stopped panicking every time a client paid late.
- She stopped saying yes to nightmare cases just because the retainer was high.
- She started taking Fridays off once a month—and the firm did not collapse.
- She showed up to work less desperate and more decisive.

Her staff noticed the difference, too.

You can't fake regulated energy. People can feel when you're leading from overflow instead of fumes.

And from that place, she could finally think clearly about **scaling**:

- Building better processes
- Hiring intentionally instead of reactively
- Investing in marketing that made sense
- Saying no to the things that didn't align

That's why owners' pay is not just a financial issue. It's a **mental health** issue and a **scale** issue.

Starving leaders don't build First-Class Firms. They build chaotic, codependent businesses that look impressive from the outside and feel miserable on the inside.

How to Start Respecting Your Vegetables

Let's bring this from theory into your world.

Here's a simple way to start, even if you feel like things are too tight right now:

1. **Figure out your current percentage.** Take your total salary + distributions + legitimate perks from last year. Divide by your total revenue. That's your current "vegetable percentage."
2. **Set a realistic next-step goal.**
    - If you're at 10%, aim for 15–18%.
    - If you're at 18%, aim for the low 20s.
    - Work your way toward that 30% mark over time.
3. **Put your salary in the budget like rent.** Stop acting like your pay is optional. It's not a tip. It's a **cost of doing business.**
4. **Say no to something that's eating better than you.** Maybe it's a subscription. Maybe it's a "vanity" expense. Maybe it's a staff role you're emotionally holding onto, but financially can't justify. Something has to give—and it can't always be you.

The New Rule

If you don't remember anything else from this chapter, remember this:

A firm where the staff, landlord, and software all eat better than the owner is not a success story. It's a red flag.

You deserve to be well-compensated, well-rested, and well-supported.

Not later. Not "once we hit that next big number."

Now.

Because the version of you who is paid fairly, mentally steady, and not checking your bank account in the dark like it's a horror movie—that's the version of you who can actually lead a First-Class Firm.

In the next chapter, we're going to talk about why your systems start breaking around the $250–300k mark and what to do about it.

But none of that will matter if we don't settle this first:

You're not the help.

You're the owner.

And it's time your compensation reflected that.

CHAPTER 3

People Over Payroll: Hiring the Right Team at the Right Time

Let's be honest: nothing will have you questioning your life choices faster than payroll week.

You open your banking app, look at the outflows, and think,

"Why does it feel like I work *for* these people instead of them working for me?"

On the flip side, not having the right people will have you:

- Drafting documents at midnight
- Answering every email yourself
- Running to FedEx like you're in a relay race

…while telling yourself, "I'll hire help when things slow down," even though you know they never actually do.

Welcome to the **L** in **C.L.I.M.B. — Labor & Leadership**.

You cannot build a First-Class Firm alone.

But you also can't build one by hiring out of panic, guilt, or vibes.

In this chapter, we're going to talk about **how to hire the right team at the right time**, using an estate planning firm as our example.

When "Help" Isn't Helping

Meet **Erica James, Esq.**

Erica owns **Legacy Path Estate Law**, a boutique estate planning firm.

- Revenue: around $750,000 a year
- Niche: busy professionals and blended families who "don't want their kids fighting over the house."
- Reputation: warm, smart, and the "explain it so my mama can understand it" lawyer

On Instagram, it looks like she has it together:

Cute office, good heels, and always some picture of her at a signing ceremony with smiling clients.

Behind the scenes?

- She's reviewing every single draft herself.
- She's in client meetings all day and then doing admin at night.
- She's missing kids' events because she's "just finishing up this one trust."
- She has one overworked assistant, a contract drafter, and a whole lot of chaos.

Erica came to me saying, "I think I need to hire another attorney."

But when we dug into it, the real problem wasn't just **needing more people**.

It was **not having the right people in the right roles**… and being scared to lead them.

Mindset Check: Are You Scared of Being the Boss?

A lot of law firm owners, especially those who grew up in struggle, have complicated feelings about being "the boss."

You might think:

- "I don't want to be like those horrible partners I used to work for."
- "My team has families; I don't want them ever to feel insecure."
- "I'd rather suffer than have to lay someone off."

So what happens?

You hire late.

You hire soft (no clear expectations).

You tolerate mediocrity because conflict makes you want to pass out.

Or, you swing the other way:

You hire fast, throw people at your problems, and now payroll is heavier than the brisket at a cookout.

Either way, your nervous system is fried.

You cannot scale a First-Class Firm if you're terrified of saying, "This is my standard."

Hiring is not just about adding people.

It's about accepting that you are building a **team**, not a friend group that happens to work near a scanner.

Every Role Either Makes Money, Protects Money, or Costs Money

To clean up Erica's situation, we started with a simple framework:

Every role in your firm should be clearly identified as:

1. **Revenue-Generating** – directly brings in money
2. **Revenue-Protecting** – makes sure you get paid and stay compliant
3. **Support** – necessary but not directly tied to dollars

Why does this matter? Because poverty rules will have you:

- Over-hiring support roles because they feel "safe."
- Under-investing in revenue-generating roles because they feel "risky."
- Keeping people on payroll who have nice personalities but no receipts in terms of results

So we mapped Erica's team:

- Erica – primary closer, primary drafter, primary everything
- Assistant – scheduling, phones, random admin
- Contract drafter – per-file basis, often late

- Bookkeeper – part-time (revenue-protecting, good move)

On paper, it looked like she "had help."

In reality, she was paying people to help her **stay stuck** at a certain level.

The Estate Planning Firm's First Three Key Hires

If you're running or building an estate planning firm, there are three core roles you want to be *very* intentional about as you grow:

1. The Intake & Client Experience Coordinator (Revenue-Generating)

This is your **front-of-house person**.

They:

- Answer calls and inquiries
- Pre-qualify leads
- Book consultations
- Follow up on proposals and unsigned engagement letters

Done well, this role **directly affects your revenue**, because:

- More qualified consults = more signed clients
- Proper follow-up = less money left on the table

Erica's assistant was trying to do this part-time, between printing documents and hunting for missing files.

We cleaned that up. Intake became a clear role with numbers attached:

- Number of consults booked
- Show-up rate
- Conversion rate after follow-ups

No more "She's really sweet, so I hope she's doing a good job."

Now we had data.

2. The Drafter / Paralegal (Revenue-Protecting)

In estate planning, you make money by:

- Designing the plan
- Drafting accurate documents
- Executing everything properly

A good drafter/paralegal is **revenue-protecting** because:

- They reduce rework and errors
- They keep matters moving
- They free you to focus on high-value tasks like strategy and signing meetings.

Erica was using a contract drafter who was often late and didn't fully understand her process. That meant she'd spend late nights "fixing it herself."

Paying twice: once in money, once in mental health.

We shifted her to a dedicated, trained drafter who was integrated into her systems—and, surprise—her stress levels dropped.

3. The Administrative Backbone (Support)

This is the role that:

- Handles scanning, filing, and organizing
- Manages mail, office logistics, and random chaos
- Supports the whole team

Support roles matter. But you can't build your whole house on them.

If your first hire is someone who "just helps with random stuff," you'll always feel like you're drowning… just with nicer folders.

Using the Plate Method to Decide Who to Hire (and When)

Remember your **food-group plate** from Chapter 1?

- Dessert – Profit
- Carbs – Tax Savings
- Vegetables – Owner Benefits
- Meat – Operating Expenses

Before we added or changed a role for Erica, we checked her **plate**.

Could the firm afford to hire or increase a role **without**:

- Touching dessert (profit)?
- Raiding carbs (tax savings)?
- Starving her vegetables (owner benefits)?

If the answer was no, we had two choices:

1. Adjust the timing or scope of the hire
2. Raise pricing / improve processes to support it

No more "I'll just squeeze it in and hope it works out."

That's not a strategy. That's stress with a name tag.

Erica's Turnaround: From Chaos Crew to Aligned Team

Here's how Erica's staffing evolved over 12–18 months:

1. **Clarified roles instead of titles.** We defined clear outcomes:
   - Intake: consults, conversion, response time
   - Drafter: turnaround time, error rates, and closure rate on matters
   - Support: keeping attorneys and paralegals operating at their highest and best use
2. **Upgraded intake to a true Client Experience Coordinator.**
   - Implemented scripts and follow-up sequences
   - Tracked metrics weekly
   - Give this person permission to *sell the value* of the firm, not just "answer questions."
3. **Brought drafting in-house with the intention.**
   - Hired one solid estate planning paralegal
   - Invested in training and documented workflows
   - Set reasonable capacity expectations so Erica wasn't editing all night
4. **Stopped apologizing for leading.** She started having real check-ins:

- "Here's what success looks like in this role."
- "Here's where you're crushing it."
- "Here's where we need improvement."

Was it uncomfortable at first?

YES.

She felt "mean" just asking for accountability.

But as she got more comfortable being the leader, not the over-functioning teammate, something shifted:

Her team respected her more.

They trusted her decisions more.

They started stepping up.

Funny how that works.

Your Nervous System and Your Next Hire

I want to name this clearly:

Hiring triggers old wounds.

If you've ever:

- Been let down when you depended on someone
- Been the "strong one" who always had to pick up the slack
- Worked for a terrible boss and promised yourself you'd never be that person

...then hiring and leading people will poke all of that.

That's why you might:

- Over-hire to avoid discomfort
- Under-hire to avoid risk
- Keep underperformers because firing them feels like betrayal

This is why mental health belongs in your hiring strategy.

You're not just putting bodies in seats.

You're building relationships that will either free you… Or drain you.

When you learn to:

- Set clear expectations
- Anchor decisions in the numbers, not your guilt
- Remember that your job is to lead, not to rescue

…your team stops being a source of constant anxiety and becomes one of your greatest assets.

Three Questions Before You Hire Anyone Else

Before you post another job ad or send another offer letter, ask yourself:

1. **Is this role revenue-generating, revenue-protecting, or support?** If you can't answer that, you're not ready to hire.
2. **Can my plate support this without stealing from dessert, carbs, or vegetables?** If the hire only works if you underpay yourself or skip tax savings, it's not sustainable.
3. **Have I defined success in this role in writing?** Not vibes. Not "help." Actual outcomes:

- "Book X consults per week"
- "Turn around drafts in X days"
- "Maintain an error rate below X%."

If you get clear on those three things, you're already ahead of 90% of small firms.

You don't need a huge team to run a First-Class Firm.

You need the **right people**, in the **right roles**, at the **right time**, backed by a CEO who isn't afraid to lead.

In the next chapter, we're going even deeper into that CEO piece—how to step fully into leadership so your firm can grow without eating you alive in the process.

CHAPTER 4

From Technician to CEO: Stop Being the Firm's Best Employee

Here's a spicy truth:

A lot of law firm "owners" are really just **overworked employees with nicer titles**.

You might have the corner office, your name on the door, maybe even a little plaque…

But if your firm cannot run, make money, and serve clients without you being in every detail?

You're not the CEO.

You're the engine.

And engines burn out.

In estate planning, especially, it's easy to hide inside the work:

- "I need to review every draft."
- "Clients expect to meet with *me*."
- "If I don't check everything, something will get missed."

It sounds like excellence.

It's actually fear.

This chapter is about becoming the **leader your firm needs** so it can scale without swallowing your whole life.

We're sticking with our estate planning friend: **Erica from Legacy Path Estate Law**.

The Day Erica Realized She Was the Bottleneck

After we cleaned up Erica's money plate and leveled up her team, she expected to feel lighter.

Instead?

She still:

- Jumped into every client email thread
- Sat in on almost every signing
- Reviewed every trust and will "just to be safe."
- Stayed late "finishing up a few things" that weren't really CEO work

When we looked at her calendar, it was wall-to-wall:

- Client meetings
- Draft reviews
- Random admin
- Sprinkle in some "CEO" tasks on weekends

I asked her one question:

"If I looked at your calendar and didn't know your title… would I think you're the CEO, or the most overworked associate?"

She didn't like me that day.

But she needed that question.

Because a First-Class Firm requires a different identity:

You can't scale as the person who does everything.

You scale as the person who builds the system that does everything.

Three Identities: Technician, Manager, CEO

Let's break it down.

Most law firm owners are constantly switching between three roles:

1. **Technician** – does the legal work
2. **Manager** – manages people and processes
3. **CEO** – sets direction, makes big decisions, protects the vision and the numbers

All three are important.

But only one of them is responsible for building a First-Class Firm.

Guess which one?

If 80–90% of your time is spent being the **technician**, your firm will always depend on you for survival.

If you want your estate planning firm to grow past a million and not break you, you need to intentionally shift more time into **Manager** and **CEO** mode.

That shift doesn't happen by accident. It happens by **design** and by **nervous system work**—because yes, your brain will fight you on this.

Why Letting Go Feels So Dangerous

For many of us who grew up in struggle, being the one who "gets it done" is our survival skill.

You were the responsible one.

The fixer.

The one people could depend on.

Now you own a firm, and that same survival skill is:

- Making you micromanage
- Keeping you from delegating
- Convincing you, "it's faster if I do it myself."
- Making you feel unsafe if you're not in every detail

That's not just a personality quirk. That's your **nervous system** saying:

"If I'm not in control, something bad will happen."

So when I tell you to start acting like the CEO and **pull back** from certain tasks, of course, that feels wrong.

Your body thinks you're abandoning your post.

But here's the reframe:

Stepping into CEO mode doesn't mean you're abandoning your firm.

It means you're finally doing the job only you can do.

How Erica Started Acting Like a CEO (Not Just Saying It)

We didn't start with a retreat or a fancy mission statement.

We started with her **week**.

Step 1: Block CEO Time (Like It's Court)

We carved out **two 2-hour CEO blocks** each week.

Non-negotiable.

During those blocks, she:

- Reviewed key numbers (cash, pipeline, signed matters)
- Checked team performance and bottlenecks
- Made decisions about pricing, offers, and capacity
- Planned marketing and strategic relationships

No client meetings.

No drafting.

No "Can I just…?" emails.

At first, her anxiety was loud.

"What if a client needs me?"

"What if my team gets stuck?"

Nothing collapsed.

Her brain slowly learned: it is safe to step back and think.

Step 2: Create "No-Fly Zones" for Low-Level Work

We identified tasks that were **beneath her pay grade**, even if she was good at them:

- Formatting documents
- Chasing down signatures
- Rescheduling consults
- Answering basic status emails

Those tasks moved to her team with clear instructions and guardrails.

Was everything done exactly like she would've done it?

No.

Was 90–95% "good enough" once standards were set?

Yes.

And that 5–10% difference was worth the time she spent getting back to functioning like a CEO.

Step 3: Measure Success Like a CEO

We shifted her focus from:

- "How many hours did I work?"

to

- "What results did the *firm* produce?"

We dialed in a few key metrics:

- Number of qualified consults
- Consultation-to-client conversion rate
- Average fee per matter
- Cycle time from consult to signed documents
- Cash in / cash out each week

When those numbers started improving, it reinforced a powerful belief:

"The less I cling to everything, the better this firm performs."

That's CEO energy.

Being the CEO *Is* a Mental Health Decision

I need you to hear this:

You being constantly overwhelmed is not a badge of honor.

It's a liability.

- Overwhelmed CEOs miss red flags.
- Exhausted CEOs avoid difficult conversations.
- Anxious CEOs make fear-based decisions that cost them money.

When you protect your time, energy, and mental space, you're not being selfish.

You're being responsible.

You're saying:

"My firm deserves a leader who can actually think clearly."

For Erica, CEO time meant:

- Sleeping better
- Snapping at her kids less
- Not feeling like she was 30 seconds from quitting the law altogether

Mental health isn't separate from your business.

It's baked into every email, every decision, every hire, every "yes" and "no."

A Simple Audit: Are You Really the CEO?

Before we move to the next part of the C.L.I.M.B. framework, I want you to do a quick check.

Look at your last week (or pull up your calendar) and ask:

1. **What percentage of my time was spent as a technician?** (Doing legal work, drafting, direct casework)
2. **What percentage was spent managing people and systems?** (Meetings with team, improving workflows, training)
3. **What percentage was spent as the CEO?** (Looking at numbers, planning, strategy, relationships)

If CEO time is under 10%, don't beat yourself up.

But don't lie to yourself either.

Name it.

Then commit to shifting it, even 5% at a time.

Because a First-Class Firm doesn't just need great legal work.

It needs **a steady, well-fed, clear-headed CEO** at the top.

That's who you're becoming.

Next up, we're going deeper into systems and infrastructure—why your firm starts to crack around $250–300k… and how to build a back-end that can actually support the First-Class life you're designing.

CHAPTER 5

Duct Tape Don't Scale: Why Your Firm Cracks Around $250K–$300K

Let's talk about that weird stage in your law firm where:

- Money is **finally** coming in
- Your calendar is full
- People know your name
- But behind the scenes... It's pure chaos with lipstick on

You've got:

- Sticky notes on your monitor
- A whiteboard with half-erased tasks
- A paralegal asking, "What's the status of...?"
- Clients are emailing, "Just checking in..." because nobody followed up

From the outside, your firm looks successful.

On the inside, it feels like you're one missed deadline away from a breakdown and a bar complaint.

Welcome to the **systems' breaking point**.

This chapter is all about the **I** in **C.L.I.M.B.** — **Infrastructure, IT, and Systems**.

Because duct tape, memory, and hustle might get you to $250K… maybe even $400K.

But if you want a **First-Class Firm** that hits seven figures **and** lets you breathe?

You're going to have to stop running your firm off vibes and Google Drive alone.

When "I Got It" Turns Into "I Can't Keep Doing This"

Let's bring back our estate planning friend, **Erica from Legacy Path Estate Law**.

When she first started, she could get away with what I call **"organized chaos"**:

- She knew every client by name
- She remembered who needed to sign what
- She could personally manage every file and every step

At $150K–$200K in revenue, that worked "fine."

Stressful, but manageable.

By the time she hit around **$300K–$400K**, here's what was happening:

- Two clients had the same first name, and she mixed up their emails
- Drafts sat for days because she kept getting pulled into consults

- Her assistant asked, "What's the process for X?" and she said the dangerous words:

"It depends… just ask me."

- She couldn't take a real vacation without Wi-Fi and a laptop

From the outside, the firm looked busy and successful.

From the inside, she felt like she was running on a hamster wheel in heels.

That's what happens when your **revenue outgrows your systems**.

Systems Are Just Decisions You Don't Want to Keep Making

Lawyers hear "systems" and think:

- Complicated software
- Big binders
- Corporate nonsense

Let's simplify.

A **system** is just:

A decision you made once… so you don't have to keep making it every day.

That's it.

- How do we schedule consults? → System
- How do we decide which leads are worth a call? → System

- What happens after a client signs an engagement letter? → System
- How do we make sure clients don't fall through the cracks? → System

No system?

Then every day, all day, you're using brainpower and willpower to answer the same questions over and over.

That's why you're tired.

You're not just doing legal work—you're doing **constant decision-making on repeat**.

Your brain is out here lifting heavy mental weights with no rest day.

The Four Core Systems Every Firm Needs (Before You Fancy It Up)

Before we talk about tech tools and automation, we need to get the **bones** right.

Every growing firm needs at least four strong systems:

1. Lead & Intake System

Question: How does someone go from "I heard about your firm" to "I'm a paying client"?

You need:

- A clear way leads come in (phone, website, referrals)
- A process for responding quickly
- Simple criteria for who qualifies for a consult

- A standard way of running that consultation
- A consistent follow-up process for people who don't sign immediately

If your answer is, "Well, it depends who picks up the phone," that's not a system. That's a gamble.

2. Matter Workflow System

Question: Once a client hires you, what happens next—every single time?

For an estate planning firm, that might look like:

1. Welcome email + onboarding
2. Questionnaire sent
3. Strategy meeting
4. Drafting
5. Review and revisions
6. Signing
7. Funding/follow-up checklist

Each step should have:

- *Who* is responsible
- *What* has to be done
- *How long* should it take

If your staff has to ask, "So what's next?" in every single case—that's a system gap.

3. Communication System

Question: How do you keep clients from blowing up your inbox?

You need:

- Standard timelines for updates ("We will update you every X weeks")
- Email templates for common touchpoints
- Clear boundaries on when and how clients can contact you
- A central place (case management, CRM) where notes actually live

Anxious clients often mean your **communication system is starving**, not just that "these people are doing too much."

4. Money Flow System

Question: How does money move through your firm—from invoice to bank to food-group accounts?

You need:

- A consistent billing rhythm (when invoices go out, how payments are collected)
- A clear process for sending reminders
- A routine for moving money into Dessert, Carbs, Vegetables, and Meat accounts
- Someone responsible for tracking it (you or your bookkeeper/CFO)

If your income is unpredictable, your stress will be predictable: high.

Your Mental Health Is Leaking Through Your Systems

Here's where we keep it real:

A lot of your system problems aren't really about time or tools.

They're about **avoidance**.

- You avoid documenting intake because you're used to just "figuring it out."
- You avoid setting policies because confrontation makes you anxious
- You avoid standardizing workflows because control makes you feel safe
- You avoid looking at money because numbers trigger old "we might not have enough" trauma

So you keep everything in your head.

And you pay for it with:

- Sleepless nights
- Forgotten tasks
- That constant low-level panic, like you left the stove on

Documented systems are not just about efficiency.

They are about **emotional safety**.

They allow you to say:

"Things are happening the way they're supposed to, even if I'm not touching everything."

That's nervous-system gold.

How Erica Started Systematizing Without Losing Her Mind

We didn't tell Erica, "You need 100 SOPs by Friday."

We started small and strategic.

Step 1: Identify the Pain Points

I asked her:

"If you had to be out of the office for 30 days and still wanted the firm to function, what would you be most worried about?"

Her list:

- New leads slipping through the cracks
- Cases stalling out in drafting
- Clients are getting mad because they didn't hear from anyone
- Money is not being collected on time

Those became our **system priorities**.

Step 2: Record What Already Works

Instead of creating everything from scratch, we captured what she already did **when things went right**.

For example:

- What does a "good" consult flow look like?
- What are the exact steps in her favorite client's matter that went smoothly?
- How did she explain complex concepts so clients actually understood?

We wrote those steps out in bullet points. Not a novel. Just enough so someone else could follow.

Step 3: Give Each System a "Home"

We didn't scatter this information across 27 tools.

We chose:

- One place for workflows (case management tool)
- One place for scripts and templates (shared drive or knowledge base)
- One person to "own" each system (Erica at first, then team leads as they grew)

Ownership matters.

If a system belongs to everyone, it belongs to no one.

Tech Is a Tool, Not a Savior

Let me say this before somebody runs off to buy three new platforms:

Software will not fix a broken thought process.

Your tech stack should **support** your systems, not replace thinking.

Ask these questions before you add a tool:

- What problem is this solving?
- What process do we already have (or need) that this will support?
- Do we have the bandwidth to actually set it up and maintain it?

I've seen firms drop $600+ a month on fancy tools they barely use…

Then tell me, "We can't afford to pay ourselves more."

That's the Meat category (operating expenses) getting bloated while your Dessert and Vegetables starve.

Tech is seasoning, not the whole meal.

Your First-Class Action Step: System Audit Lite

Before you turn the page, do this quick exercise.

Grab a piece of paper—or open a doc—and write down the four core systems:

1. Lead & Intake
2. Matter Workflow
3. Communication
4. Money Flow

Next to each one, rate yourself from **1 to 5**:

- **1** = Pure chaos, lives in my head
- **3** = Some structure, inconsistent
- **5** = Documented, team follows it, I could step away, and it would still run

Where are you leaking energy?

Where is your anxiety the highest?

Start there.

Because building a First-Class Firm isn't about working harder.

It's about building **infrastructure** that can carry the weight of your vision—without breaking your back in the process.

In the next chapter, we'll zoom in on your tech and tools—the "IT" piece of C.L.I.M.B.—and talk about what actually belongs in a law firm's tech stack (and what needs to go in the trash).

CHAPTER 6

Click Less, Collect More: Building a Tech Stack That Works for You (Not the Other Way Around)

Can we be honest for a second?

A lot of law firm tech stacks look like this:

- Three different CRMs you "meant to try"
- Two calendar tools
- A case management system nobody uses properly
- Fifteen Chrome tabs are permanently pinned "for later."
- Subscriptions you only remember exist when the card gets charged

And then, when I bring up paying yourself more, you're like:

"We *would*… but these software costs are killing us."

Let's call it what it is:

You don't have a tech stack.

You have a **tech pile**.

This chapter is about the "IT" side of **Infrastructure** in your C.L.I.M.B. framework—how to use tools to simplify your life, protect your brain, and support a First-Class Firm… without turning your operating expenses into an all-you-can-eat buffet.

When Notifications Become Another Job

We left **Erica at Legacy Path Estate Law,** starting to build systems.

She got:

- A better intake process
- A clearer workflow for estate planning matters
- Some boundaries around her CEO time

On paper, things were cleaner.

But her day still felt like this:

- Ping. Email.
- Ding. Case management alert.
- Pop-up. Internal chat.
- Text. "Hey, did you see my email?"

By 11 a.m., she was overstimulated and underproductive.

Here's the part we don't talk about enough:

A chaotic tech environment is a mental health issue, not just an efficiency issue.

All those notifications?

They're little mini-adrenaline hits.

Your brain stays in **fight-or-flight mode**, never getting enough time to think deeply or lead.

You can't build a First-Class Firm if your nervous system is being jumped by your tech all day.

So, we had to clean her digital house.

Your Tech Should Serve Your Systems, Not Replace Them

Remember from the last chapter:

A **system** is just a decision you made once, so you don't have to keep making it.

Tech is how you **deliver** that decision consistently.

But here's where a lot of law firms go wrong:

- They buy software before they define the process
- They expect tools to magically "fix" chaos
- They copy what another firm uses without checking if it matches their model

We flipped the script with Erica, and we're going to flip it for you, too.

Rule #1:

Identify the process first.

Add tech second.

The Five Jobs Your Tech Stack Must Cover

You do *not* need 37 tools.

You need the right tools that cover the right **jobs**.

Most small to mid-sized firms need tech that handles at least five core jobs:

1. **Client & Case Management**
2. **Communication & Scheduling**
3. **Money & Metrics**
4. **Document Creation & Storage**
5. **Marketing & Follow-Up**

Let's walk through them.

1. Client & Case Management: Your Digital Command Center

This is where:

- Matters live
- Tasks are assigned
- Deadlines are tracked
- Notes are stored

If you're still running your firm from:

- Email
- A spreadsheet
- The "search" bar in your inbox

...you're not just making your life harder—you're increasing your anxiety.

Why?

Because your brain knows things are falling through the cracks, even if you can't see them yet.

A good case management system should:

- Show you **what needs to be done today**
- Show you **who is responsible**
- Make it easy to see **where each case is in the pipeline**

If your system doesn't do that, or you're not using it that way, the tool isn't helping you—it's just billing you.

2. Communication & Scheduling: Fewer Back-and-Forths, More Boundaries

Inbox chaos is one of the biggest mental health drains for lawyers.

Your tech here should:

- Make it easy for clients to **book consults and calls** without ten emails
- Give you a way to send **templated updates,** so you're not rewriting the same email twenty times
- Keep staff from using your personal cell for every minor question

This might look like:

- A booking link tied to your calendar
- Standard email templates are stored where your team can access them
- Internal chat or communication tools used with clear rules (not just "ping me anytime")

The goal is **fewer decisions**, not fancier features.

3. Money & Metrics: Protecting Your Peace (and Your Profit)

Money tools should do two major things:

- Help you **collect money efficiently**
- Help you **see what's really going on**

This might include:

- A billing/invoicing platform (or built-in billing in your case management)
- Accounting software
- A simple reporting dashboard (even if it's a monthly spreadsheet)

If you avoid logging into your financial tools because they make you anxious, that's a problem—not a personality trait.

You need a setup where:

- You can see cash in/cash out
- You know which matters are paid, behind, or underpriced
- It's easy to move money into your Dessert, Carbs, Vegetables, and Meat accounts

If your tech makes that **harder**, not easier? Time to reevaluate.

4. Document Creation & Storage: Stop Hunting for Things Like You Lost Your Keys

In an estate planning firm, documents are your product.

Your tech should make it easy to:

- Use templates without reinventing the wheel

- Version documents without confusion
- Store everything in a clear folder or matter structure

If every draft is called "Smith Trust FINAL v7 REALLY FINAL," your tech is not the only problem—but it can definitely help.

Clear, consistent document workflows reduce error, save time, and lower that *"Did we miss something?"* anxiety that keeps you up at night.

5. Marketing & Follow-Up: Don't Make Your Future Clients Chase You

You can do all the networking, speaking, and posting in the world—but if you don't have a way to **capture and follow up**, you're just doing performance art.

At a minimum, your tech should support:

- A simple way to collect leads (website forms, QR codes, landing pages)
- A list (email or CRM) where leads actually *live*
- A consistent follow-up process—automated where possible

This doesn't have to be complicated.

Even a basic email platform can help you:

- Nurture leads
- Follow up with people who attended a webinar or downloaded a guide
- Stay in front of your audience without manually sending every message

Remember: **Quiet prospects aren't always uninterested.**

Sometimes they're just busy. Your system's job is to keep the conversation going.

How We Put Erica's Tech on a Diet

Here's what we did for Legacy Path Estate Law:

1. **Listed every tool she was paying for.** CRM, email tools, survey tools, scheduler, case management, random apps.
2. **Asked two questions for each:**
    - What job is this tool doing?
    - Are we actually using it for that job?
3. **Cut anything that:**
    - Overlapped with another tool
    - It was only being used at 10% capacity
    - No one could explain the purpose of ("I just thought it might help…")

We dropped a few hundred dollars a month in software fees—without losing any real capability.

Then we:

- Committed to using her case management system as the **single source of truth** for matters
- Standardized client communication templates and stored them in one place
- Set up basic automation for:
    - Appointment confirmations
    - Post-consult follow-up

- "We haven't heard from you," nudges

Nothing wild.

No heavy coding.

Just intention.

Within a few months:

- Fewer things fell through the cracks
- Her team stopped asking, "Where do I find…?" every hour
- She felt **less mentally cluttered**, which translated into better leadership choices

Don't Let Shiny Objects Steal Your Vegetables

Every time a new tech tool pops up promising to "10x your firm," remember this:

That subscription will be paid from your Meat account, and if you're not careful, it will start nibbling at your Vegetables and Dessert.

Before you buy something new, ask:

1. **What system is this supporting?** (If the answer is "I don't know yet," pause.)
2. **What will we stop using if we add this?** (Something has to go, or you're just piling.)
3. **What result will tell us that this tool is worth it?** (More consults? Faster drafting? Fewer no-shows?)

Talk about it with your team.

Document the decision.

Set a calendar reminder three months out: "Review whether [Tool] is earning its seat at the table."

Grown firm decisions only.

Your First-Class Action Step: Simplify to Scale

Before you move to the next chapter, I want you to do a quick tech detox check.

Write down:

- Every tool you pay for monthly or annually
- What is the main job each one is supposed to do
- Whether that job is actually getting done

Then choose **one**:

- One tool to eliminate

or

- One tool to recommit to using properly (and schedule time to set it up right)

Your goal is not to have the fanciest tech stack.

Your goal is to have a **calm brain, a clear system, and a firm that runs smoothly enough that you can actually enjoy the dessert you're working so hard to earn.**

In the next chapter, we're moving into the **M** of C.L.I.M.B.—Marketing, Visibility, and Business Development—so you can bring in more of the *right* clients at the *right* price, without burning yourself out trying to be everywhere at once.

CHAPTER 7

Be Loud, Get Booked: Becoming the Most Visible Lawyer in Your Market

Let's go ahead and say the quiet part out loud:

There are lawyers in your city right now who are **less skilled than you**, doing **sloppier work than you**, charging **more than you**...

...and they are booked out.

Not because they're better lawyers.

Because they're better at being **seen**.

Meanwhile, you're over here like, "My work should speak for itself."

Baby, your work doesn't have Wi-Fi.

It's not getting on Instagram.

It's not going to networking events for you.

In the **C.L.I.M.B.** framework, we've handled your **Cash**, your **Labor**, and your **Infrastructure**.

Now we're stepping into the **M**:

Marketing, Visibility, and Business Development.

Because you cannot build a First-Class Firm if the only people who know how amazing you are are your mama, your best friend, and the people already on your docket.

Visibility Is Not Vanity — It's Oxygen

A lot of lawyers—especially those who grew up in "don't draw attention to yourself" households—have a complicated relationship with visibility.

You may be carrying beliefs like:

- "If I promote myself, I'm being cocky."
- "Real professionals don't have to market like that."
- "I don't want people to think I'm chasing clout."

So you keep your head down, do good work, and wonder why your referral pipeline feels like it's on dial-up.

Let's reframe.

Visibility is not vanity. Visibility is **oxygen** for your business.

If people can't find you, they can't pay you.

If people don't remember you, they won't refer to you.

If people don't understand what you do, they'll keep calling you for the wrong things—or not at all.

Visibility, done right, is:

- You are educating your community
- You're giving people language for the problems they've been ignoring

- You are showing up as a trusted guide, not a desperate salesperson

That's not clout-chasing.

That's leadership.

Meet The Quiet Genius: The PI Lawyer Nobody Knows

Let's switch our example for a minute and talk about **Andre Lewis**, a composite of several personal injury lawyers I've worked with.

Andre runs **Lewis Justice Group**, a small PI firm focusing on car accidents and trucking cases.

Here's his reality:

- He's actually really good in the courtroom
- His clients who *do* find him love him
- He cares deeply about his community

But…

- His website looks like it was made on dial-up
- He posts on social media twice a month… maybe
- His "marketing plan" is basically, "I hope people refer to me."

Meanwhile, down the street, there's a firm with catchy billboards, wild commercials, and a jingle stuck in everybody's head like that one song from childhood you can't un-hear.

Is that firm better? Not necessarily.

But if you ask the average person in that city, "Who's a good injury lawyer?" guess whose names they're going to say?

Not the quiet genius.

The ones they **see** and **hear** the most.

That's the power of omnipresence.

Omnipresence: Be Everywhere (Without Being Everywhere)

Now, I'm not saying you need to be on every platform doing dances and pointing at captions.

What I *am* saying is this:

Your ideal clients should feel like "you're everywhere" **in their world**.

That might mean:

- They see you when they scroll Facebook or Instagram
- They hear about you at local events
- Your name comes up in certain professional circles
- When they Google their problem, *you* show up with answers

You don't need to be viral.

You need to be **consistent** and **strategic**.

Omnipresence isn't about exhausting yourself.

It's about building systems so your content, relationships, and presence keep working even when you're off living your First-Class life.

The Poverty Mindset Hiding in Your Marketing

Let's keep it real: most marketing problems aren't really about "not knowing what to post."

They're about **fear** and **old money stories**.

Some of the things I hear:

- "I don't want people to think I'm doing too much."
- "What if other lawyers judge me?"
- "What if I post and nobody engages? I'll feel stupid."
- "I grew up being told to stay humble and not brag."

Sound familiar?

That's not just shyness.

That's survival-mode messaging from childhood:

"Don't draw attention. Don't make noise. Don't be 'too much.'"

But here's the thing:

You are not that kid anymore.

You are a law firm owner trying to build a million-dollar, First-Class Firm.

The rules are different at this level.

Staying invisible doesn't keep you safe.

It keeps you stuck.

The Four Pillars of First-Class Visibility

You don't need to reinvent yourself as a full-time influencer. You need a **visibility engine** made of four pillars:

1. **Content** – What you say
2. **Platform** – Where you say it
3. **People** – Who you connect with
4. **Proof** – Why they should trust you

Let's break it down.

1. Content: Say What They're Afraid to Google

Content is just you answering the questions your ideal clients are already asking—in their heads, in their group chats, in their late-night panic scroll.

For example:

- Estate planning: "Will my kids be okay if something happens to me?"
- PI: "Do I *really* need a lawyer after this accident?"
- Family law: "How do I protect myself financially if we divorce?"

Good content:

- Names the fear
- Gives clarity
- Offers a next step

You don't have to give away the whole strategy.

You have to show, "I understand your problem, and I know what to do next."

Content is not about sounding smart.

It's about being **useful**.

2. Platform: Pick Your Main Stage

Trying to do **everything** is a trauma response dressed up as productivity.

Choose:

- One **primary platform** where you show up consistently (e.g., Facebook, Instagram, LinkedIn, YouTube)
- One **secondary platform** for repurposed content
- One **offline lane** (networking, speaking, bar associations, community orgs)

For Andre, the PI lawyer, we chose:

- Primary: Facebook (where his community actually hangs out)
- Secondary: Instagram (repurposed clips and posts)
- Offline: Local medical providers, body shops, and community events

For you, that combination might look different.

The point is: **intention over exhaustion**.

3. People: Relationships > Random Followers

You do not need 100,000 followers to have a million-dollar firm.

You need the **right people** who:

- Need your services
- Can refer clients to you
- Can put you in front of rooms you want to be in

This means thinking strategically about:

- Therapists, financial advisors, and realtors for estate planning and family law
- Doctors, chiropractors, and mechanics for personal injury
- Business owners and leaders for employment or business law

Your visibility plan should include **time and systems** for:

- Nurturing these relationships
- Checking in
- Sending value (resources, intros, co-hosted events)

Visibility isn't just marketing. It's **business development.**

4. Proof: Show the Receipts

In a noisy market, people are asking:

"Why you?"

Your job is to answer that without sounding desperate or arrogant.

Proof can look like:

- Testimonials (with permission)
- Case outcomes (shared ethically and within bar rules)

- Speaking engagements
- Media features
- Before/after stories (even anonymized composites)

This is where you weave in:

- "Here's how we helped a blended family avoid chaos after a sudden loss."
- "Here's how a client went from lowball offer to fair settlement."

Again, not bragging.

Documenting impact.

How Andre Went From Invisible to In-Demand

For Andre, the PI lawyer, we built a simple visibility engine:

1. **Content Plan**
    - Weekly short videos explaining common PI myths
    - Simple carousel posts like "3 Things to Do Right After a Car Wreck."
    - Monthly "Case Story (Without the Legalese)" posts
2. **Platform Focus**
    - Posted consistently on Facebook
    - Reused the same content on Instagram
    - Uploaded key videos to YouTube for search
3. **People Strategy**
    - Built a small list of local chiropractors, doctors, and shops

- Sent them useful resources for patients
- Checked in quarterly with coffee meetings or quick calls

4. **Proof**

- Asked happy clients for Google reviews
- Shared anonymized "win" stories once or twice a month
- Showed up on a local podcast to talk about protecting your rights after accidents

Within a year:

- His consults became more consistent
- People started saying, "I feel like I see you everywhere."
- His **average case value** went up because better clients were finding him
- He felt less like he was shouting into the void and more like he was leading the conversation

Nothing overnight.

No viral moment.

Just consistent, aligned marketing that matched his mission.

Protecting Your Mental Health While You Show Up

Here's what I need you to remember:

You can show up without sacrificing your sanity.

A few guidelines:

- **Batch content.** Record or write in focused blocks, not randomly at 11 p.m.

- **Set boundaries.** You don't have to reply to every troll or answer DMs at midnight.
- **Separate performance from worth.** A low-like post does not mean you're not good at what you do.
- **Get support.** A VA or marketing assistant can help execute your visibility plan so you don't have to do it all yourself.

You're allowed to be visible **and** grounded.

Visible **and** private about what matters.

Visible **and** selective about what you engage with.

Your First-Class Action Step: Start Your Visibility Engine

Before you move on, answer these three questions:

1. **Who is my ideal client, really, and what keeps them up at night?** (Write down at least 3 fears or questions they have.)
2. **Where do they actually spend their attention?** (Online and offline.)
3. **What is one way I can show up consistently for the next 90 days?** (One platform + one offline channel.)

Then commit.

Not to perfection.

Not going viral.

Commit to being **findable**, **helpful**, and **present**.

Because a First-Class Firm is not built in the shadows.

It's built by a lawyer who is willing to step into the light, tell the truth, and let the people who need them know:

"I'm here, I understand, and I can help."

CHAPTER 8

Charge Like a First-Class Firm: Elevating Your Average Client Value

Let's start with a little gut punch:

If your firm is busy but your bank account still looks malnourished,

You don't have a marketing problem.

You have a **pricing and packaging problem**.

You do not get to a First-Class Firm by being the **discount option** in your market.

You get there by:

- Solving real problems deeply
- Positioning yourself as the guide, not a commodity
- Charging in a way that actually supports the life you're building

A million dollars in revenue with broke pricing is just a **fancy struggle**.

We're not doing fancy struggles.

This chapter is about raising your **average client value**—so you can work with better-fit clients, do better work, and eat the dessert you've been talking about.

When "Affordable" Becomes "Exhausted"

Meet **Tanya Rivera, Esq.** (another composite character).

Tanya owns **Rivera Legacy Planning**, an estate planning firm serving middle-income and upper-middle-income families.

Her old model:

- Wills starting at $750
- Basic revocable trusts around $1,500–$2,000
- Almost everything was "custom," which meant everything was chaos

Her calendar stayed full.

But:

- She was on Zoom and in meetings constantly
- Clients nitpicked invoices
- She felt guilty raising prices because "these families really need help."
- By the time she paid staff and expenses, her plate was… let's say, mostly meat and no dessert.

On paper, she was "affordable."

In reality, she was **exhausted** and underpaid.

That's not generosity.

That's self-neglect with nice branding.

The Poverty Mindset Hiding in Your Pricing

Let's unpack why so many law firm owners undercharge—even when they "know better" in their heads.

For a lot of us who grew up in or near poverty, money came with messages like:

- "Don't be greedy."
- "People like us should just be grateful."
- "Good people help, even if they don't have much."

You bring that into your law firm and suddenly:

- You feel guilty charging what your service is worth
- You discount without being asked
- You over-deliver like you're auditioning for sainthood
- You resent clients who demand a lot while paying a little

Underpricing isn't just a strategy error.

It's a **trauma response**.

Your brain is trying to prove, "I'm not like those money-hungry people,"

So you swing to the other extreme and build a firm that takes care of everyone but you.

We're not doing that anymore.

Average Client Value: The Metric You're Ignoring

Most firm owners obsess over the **number of clients**.

"How many new matters did we open?"

"How many leads did we get?"

Important, yes. But not complete.

You also need to ask:

"How much is each client worth to the firm on average?"

Average Client Value (ACV) is:

Total revenue for a period ÷ total number of matters opened

If you made $600,000 from 200 matters last year, your ACV is $3,000.

If you could serve 150 matters next year at $4,000 ACV?

Same energy, more money, less chaos.

The fastest path to a First-Class Firm isn't always **more clients**.

Sometimes it's **better for clients at better pricing**.

When Your Pricing Starves Your Plate

Let's bring the food groups back:

- **Dessert** – Profit (5%+)
- **Carbs** – Tax Savings (10%)
- **Vegetables** – Owner Benefits (30%+ target)
- **Meat** – Operating Expenses (what's left)

If your pricing is too low:

- Dessert disappears first
- Then veggies get cut (you stop paying yourself)
- Then carbs get ignored (hello tax stress)

- Meat stays bloated because you're trying to "keep up" with the caseload

Low prices **don't just hurt your revenue**.

They throw your entire plate out of balance and keep your nervous system stressed.

Proper pricing is not just numbers.

It's **mental health protection**.

How Tanya Triple-Step Upgraded Her Fees

When Tanya and I dug into her numbers, we realized something wild:

Her clients weren't actually price shopping.

They:

- Wanted someone who could explain things clearly
- Wanted to avoid family drama and court
- Wanted peace of mind, not the cheapest option

She was the one leading with affordability, not them.

Here's how we leveled her up.

Step 1: Define Clear Tiers

We created three core estate planning packages:

1. **Foundation Plan** – For simple situations
2. **Protection Plan** – For families with kids, property, and more complexity

3. **Legacy Plan** – For higher-net-worth or blended families needing deeper planning

Each tier had:

- Clear features
- Clear outcomes
- A clear price

No more "it depends" on everything.

No more reinventing the wheel for each client.

Step 2: Raise Prices to Match Reality

We moved her:

- From $1,500 trusts to packages starting closer to $3,500 and going up from there
- From charging for documents to charging for **comprehensive planning**

She was terrified.

We practiced:

- Saying the numbers out loud without apologizing
- Explaining value in terms that clients actually cared about
- Holding silence after stating the price (instead of nervously discounting her own quote)

The first time a client said, "Okay, that makes sense,"

She almost fell out of her chair.

That wasn't a pricing issue.

That was a **self-worth issue**.

Step 3: Protect Her Energy with Better Fit Clients

As prices rose:

- Some people self-selected out (and that was fine)
- Fewer clients treated her like a commodity
- She had space to actually **think**, not just grind

Her average client value went up.

Her stress went down.

And yes, she had to sit with the discomfort of not being "the cheap option" anymore.

But guess what the other side of that discomfort is called?

First-Class.

Practical Ways to Elevate Your Average Client Value

You don't have to triple your fees tomorrow.

But you do need to **stop building a firm for everybody** and start building it for the people who are ready and able to value your work.

Here are a few ways to raise your ACV without losing your mind:

1. Raise Your Floor

If you're a busy firm and constantly overwhelmed, your lowest fee is probably too low.

- Set a **minimum fee** you will not go under

- Stop offering the cheapest options you resent delivering
- Let your "no" protect your energy and make room for better "yeses."

2. Add Depth, Not Just Documents

Shift from selling **paper** to selling **outcomes**.

Instead of:

"We'll draft a trust and will for you."

Try:

"We'll create a full plan so that if you become incapacitated or pass away, your family doesn't have to fight, guess, or go to court unnecessarily."

Outcome-based language supports value-based pricing.

3. Use Payment Options, Not Desperation Discounts

If affordability is truly a barrier for some ideal clients,

use:

- Payment plans
- Phased services
- Financing options (where appropriate)

Don't panic-discount in the room because someone flinched at the price.

4. Measure It

Every quarter, track:

- Total revenue

- Number of new matters
- Your ACV (revenue ÷ matters)

Then ask:

- "What's one adjustment we can make to increase this number without burning me out?"

Small, consistent upgrades compound.

Your Nervous System Will Try to Talk You Out of This

Let's be real.

When you start charging more:

- Old guilt will tap you on the shoulder
- You'll worry, "What will people think?"
- You'll have a slow week, and your brain will scream, "Drop the prices!"

That's your survival brain—**not** your CEO brain—talking.

Survival brain remembers:

- Not having enough
- Being judged
- Being told, "Who do you think you are?"

The CEO's brain knows:

- You are building a firm that supports your life
- You do excellent work that prevents chaos

- You deserve to be well-compensated for the value you provide

You have to decide which voice runs your firm.

Your First-Class Action Step: One Bold Move

Before you move on, choose **one** of these and commit:

- Raise your minimum fee on your most popular service by 10–20%
- Create a simple three-tier package structure instead of bespoke pricing for everyone
- Stop offering your cheapest, most draining service after this month

Write it down.

Tell someone on your team.

Give your nervous system time to adjust.

Because here's the truth:

You can't build a First-Class Firm on coach-flight pricing and Greyhound boundaries.

You deserve dessert.

You deserve full vegetables.

You deserve carbs without panic.

And your meat category will be just fine when your pricing starts reflecting your worth.

In the next chapter, we're going to talk about **networking and partnerships**—how to turn relationships into consistent revenue so you're not depending solely on ads, algorithms, or "hoping for referrals" to hit your goals.

CHAPTER 9

Rooms, Relationships, and Revenue: Networking That Actually Moves the Needle

Let's go ahead and drag this one to the light:

A lot of lawyers say they "hate networking"…

But what they really hate is **awkward small talk, fake smiles, and leaving events with nothing but a sad cheese cube and a stack of useless business cards.**

You don't hate people.

You hate **pointless** people-ing.

On top of that, if you grew up with any social anxiety, being the quiet kid, or being told "don't let people in our business," walking into a room full of strangers to "promote yourself" can feel like a full-on nervous system attack.

But here's the truth:

You cannot build a First-Class Firm in isolation.

Your next level lives in **rooms and relationships** you're not in yet.

This chapter is about **strategic networking and partnerships**—so you're not just "getting your name out," you're building a **referral ecosystem** that consistently feeds your Dessert, Carbs, Vegetables, and Meat.

Why Most Networking Doesn't Work

Most lawyers approach networking like this:

- Show up late to a random event
- Talk to whoever's standing near the food
- Hand out cards like Halloween candy
- Go home, toss other people's cards in a drawer
- Never follow up

Then say, "Networking doesn't work for me."

No, *that* doesn't work for you.

Let's call it what it is: **Activity without strategy**.

You don't need more events. You need **intentional connections**.

And to get those, you have to shift your mindset from:

"How many people can I meet?"

To

"Who do I need to build real relationships with?"

Meet the Event Hopper: Busy, Visible… and Broke

Let me introduce you to **Carla Nguyen, Esq.** (you know the drill—composite attorney).

Carla owns a small **employment law firm** focused on wrongful termination and workplace discrimination.

If there was an event in her city, she was there:

- Bar association mixers
- Chamber of Commerce breakfasts
- Women's leadership luncheons
- "Young professionals" meetups, even though she was pushing 40 and tired

Her calendar stayed packed with "networking."

Her bank account? Not so much.

When we looked at where her clients were actually coming from, we found something embarrassing (her words, not mine):

Maybe **5–10%** were from all those events.

Most of her best cases came from:

- Two therapists who regularly referred their burned-out, mistreated clients
- One business lawyer sent over conflicts
- One former opposing counsel who respected her work

Four relationships… doing more than forty events.

That's the power of **focus**.

The Poverty Mindset Behind "Being Everywhere"

Here's where we keep it real:

Running around to everything and saying yes to every invitation is often a **scarcity response**.

Deep down, the story sounds like:

- "If I'm not everywhere, I'll miss out."
- "If I stop showing up, people will forget me."
- "I have to earn every opportunity with hustle."

That's the same energy as:

- Hoarding clients instead of raising prices
- Hoarding tasks instead of delegating
- Hoarding control instead of trusting systems

We don't hoard in a First-Class Firm.

We **choose**.

Your nervous system might think, "More = safer."

Your CEO brain needs to say, "Aligned = sustainable."

Strategic Networking: The Power of Your Top 20

Instead of chasing every room, I want you to build a **Top 20 List**:

20 people or categories of people who, if you had strong relationships with them, could consistently send you your **ideal clients**.

For example, an estate planning firm's Top 20 might include:

- Financial advisors
- CPAs
- Real estate agents
- Therapists who work with blended families
- Past clients who are connectors

A personal injury firm's Top 20 might include:

- Chiropractors
- Primary care doctors
- Body shops
- Insurance agents
- Community leaders

A family law firm's Top 20 might include:

- Therapists and counselors
- Divorce coaches
- Realtors
- Loan officers
- Mediators

Each of these isn't just "a person."

They're a **pipeline**.

If each one refers just 3–5 ideal clients a year?

Your firm doesn't have a leads problem ever again.

Relationships, Not Transactions

We had Carla (the employment lawyer) do this exercise.

Her list included:

- Mental health professionals
- HR consultants
- Business attorneys
- A few organizers of key community events

Then we had to deal with her other survival script:

"I don't want to bother people or feel like I'm using them."

Common. Especially if you grew up feeling like a burden anytime you needed help.

So here's the reframe:

Strategic relationships are not about **using** people.

They're about **creating mutual value**.

Instead of sliding into people's inboxes like, "Hey, send me cases," we built a different approach:

- **Learn** what they need
- **Offer** resources that make them look good to their clients
- **Introduce** them to others who can help them
- **Invite** collaboration (webinars, workshops, content)

Now, you're not just another lawyer with a card.

You're a **partner**.

The Simple Partnership Framework (Without Being Awkward)

Here's an easy three-step process you can use with any potential referral partner:

Step 1: Reach Out With Respect

Keep it light and specific. For example:

"Hey [Name], I work with [type of clients] who are often also dealing with [issues in their world]. I'd love to learn more about what you're seeing and see if there's a way we can support each other's clients better."

Notice:

- You're not begging for referrals
- You're not leading with "what can you do for me?"
- You're offering a conversation about mutual client care

Step 2: Listen More Than You Talk

On the call or coffee:

- Ask about **their** work
- Ask what challenges their clients face
- Ask what kind of resources would help them serve better

You'll often find natural overlap:

- Therapists with clients facing divorce
- Doctors with injured patients are unsure about calling a lawyer
- CPAs with clients fumbling with estate planning or business structure

Take notes. Ask, "What would make it easier for you to refer when it makes sense?"

Step 3: Co-Create Something Small and Simple

Instead of "Send me cases," try:

- A short PDF or one-page guide they can share with clients

- A Q&A webinar for their audience
- An email template they can use when introducing you

You're making it **easy** and **comfortable** for them to connect people to you.

Over time, as you show up consistently and take good care of the people they send?

Trust grows. Referrals follow.

Your Nervous System and the Room

For some of you, the hardest part isn't the emails or the strategy.

It's **walking into the room.**

If you:

- Get social anxiety
- Feel drained after events
- Replay every awkward conversation in your head for 3 days

...you're not broken. You're human.

Here are a few ways to protect your mental health while you build your First-Class network:

- **Limit your capacity.** Decide in advance: "I'll go to 2 quality events a month," not 7.
- **Go with a purpose.** Set an intention: "I want to genuinely connect with 3 people who serve [your ideal clients]."

- **Have exit plans.** It's okay to leave once you've hit your objective. You don't have to close the bar.
- **Regulate before and after.** Deep breaths in the car. Music that calms you. A walk afterward. Take care of your nervous system like you take care of your calendar.

A regulated person will always network better than a frazzled you.

Carla's Shift: Fewer Rooms, More Revenue

Once Carla shifted from "event hopping" to **relationship building**, her life changed.

She:

- Stopped going to every random mixer
- Focused on quarterly touchpoints with her Top 20
- Co-hosted a webinar with a therapist on "Your Rights at Work When You're Being Targeted."
- Partnered with an HR consultant for training, where she offered a free resource at the end

Within a year:

- She cut her "networking time" in half
- Her **best** cases came from just 7–8 key relationships
- She felt less drained and more connected
- Her revenue increased—but more importantly, the work felt aligned

That's networking that moves the needle.

Your First-Class Action Step: Build Your Top 20

Before you close this chapter, I want you to do this:

1. **Write down 3–5 characteristics of your ideal client.** (Practice area + personality + life situation.)
2. **List 10–20 people or professions who:**
    - Already see those clients
    - Already have their trust
    - Could naturally refer them to you when the time is right
3. **Circle 5 names or categories to start with.** Those are your first outreach targets for the next 60–90 days.

Remember:

You're not "bothering" people.

You're building bridges that help *your* clients and *your* firm thrive.

A First-Class Firm doesn't sit back and hope the phone rings.

It builds a network so strong that even when the algorithms trip and the ads slow down,

The referrals keep coming.

And you?

You get to enjoy your dessert knowing you are deeply, strategically connected.

CHAPTER 10

Million-Dollar Decisions: Designing a Firm That Actually Works

Let's clear something up:

There's a **big** difference between:

- A firm that *hits* a million dollars in revenue
- And a firm that is **built** to be a million-dollar, First-Class Firm

One is "We had a crazy year."

The other is "This is how our machine runs."

You don't get a First-Class Firm by accident.

You get it by making **million-dollar decisions** on purpose.

Not just, "Should I hire this paralegal?"

But:

- Should we even offer this service?
- Is this the right type of client for our model?
- Does this fee structure make sense?

- Can this firm support my Dessert, Carbs, Vegetables, and Meat for the *long haul*?

That's business modeling.

And most law firm owners avoid it like it's a root canal with no anesthesia.

You Don't Just Have a Firm. You Have a Business Model.

Your **business model** is:

How your firm makes money, who it makes money from, and what it costs you—time, money, and energy—to deliver that.

Whether you've thought about it or not, you already have a business model.

Maybe it looks like this:

- **Practice areas:** "A little bit of everything."
- **Clients:** Whoever shows up and can pay *something*
- **Pricing:** Whatever sounds "reasonable" in the moment
- **Delivery:** You're doing way too much of the work

That's not a model.

That's a survival strategy with a letterhead.

We're going to change that.

Meet the "Yes to Everything" Firm

Let's talk about **Marcus Hill, Esq.** – composite criminal defense and family law attorney.

His firm, **Hill Law Group**, was doing just over $900,000 in annual revenue.

On paper, great.

In reality, a mess:

- He handled criminal defense, family law, some traffic, a little landlord/tenant "if they needed it," and the occasional random civil matter
- Half his cases were low-fee, high-drama
- The other half was decent, but he was constantly pushed back because he was drowning in everything else.
- His staff never knew what was coming next: "Are we doing a motion or a divorce petition or a payment plan or…?"

His schedule was chaotic.

His brain was fried.

His Dessert and Vegetables accounts were underfed, but the Meat (operating expenses) was full and happy.

When I asked him, "What's your business model?"

He said, "We help people in crisis."

That's noble.

But it's not a model.

Poverty Rules in a Million-Dollar Firm

When we unpacked Marcus's decisions, there was a common theme:

"I don't want to turn people away."

Underneath that?

- "What if the phone stops ringing?"
- "Growing up, we took whatever we could get."
- "Saying no feels like I'm being ungrateful."

So he said yes to:

- Cases that didn't fit
- Clients who had *some* money but not enough
- Court appointments that drained his time and energy

He built a business model that matched his **past**, not his **goals**.

That's what happens when poverty rules follow you into your firm:

- You think focus is "risky."
- You think boundaries are "mean."
- You think raising standards is "forgetting where you came from."

No.

Focus, boundaries, and standards are how you **honor** where you came from—by not recreating struggle in a place that was supposed to set you free.

The Five Levers of a First-Class Business Model

To turn Marcus's situation around—and yours—we pulled on five key levers.

You can use these in any practice area.

1. Case Mix: What You Actually Offer

Not every matter belongs in your firm.

Ask:

- Which case types are **profitable, predictable, and energizing**?
- Which ones are **draining, unpredictable, and low-value**?

For Marcus, we realized:

- His **higher-value divorces and serious criminal matters** brought in most of the revenue
- Traffic and random low-level stuff ate his time, cluttered the calendar, and stressed him out

So we made a decision:

No more "whatever walks in the door."

The model is built around **fewer, better cases**.

That one decision changed everything.

2. Pricing Structure: How You Get Paid

Hourly for everything is not always the move.

Flat fees for everything can also be a problem if you don't know your numbers.

The point is alignment:

- Does this fee structure make sense for **this** type of work?
- Does it support your food groups (Dessert, Carbs, Vegetables, Meat)?

For example:

- Flat fees for certain predictable stages of a case
- Hybrid models (flat for pre-trial, hourly, or a different fee for trial)
- Clear retainers and replenishment rules in family law or criminal defense

Million-dollar decisions look like:

"I'm not going to let people drag me through 12 months of chaos for a fee that only makes sense for 3."

3. Delivery Model: Who Does the Work

You are not the only qualified human in your building.

Ask:

- Which parts of the work *must* be done by an attorney?
- Which parts can be done by a paralegal, assistant, or automation?
- Where are you holding onto tasks because of ego or anxiety?

Your business model should include leverage:

- Standard processes a paralegal can follow
- Templates instead of reinventing the wheel

- Intake and screening handled by trained staff, not you

Every hour you spend on work beneath your pay grade is your model leaking profit **and** mental health.

4. Capacity: How Much You Can Logically Handle

You are not a limitless resource.

A grown, First-Class business model asks:

- How many active cases can each attorney/paralegal handle and still do quality work?
- How many new matters per month can your firm onboard without chaos?
- What happens if you hit that limit—do you raise prices, hire, or waitlist?

Marcus had never asked those questions.

He just kept saying yes.

Once we defined capacity, we could:

- Plan hiring
- Adjust pricing when demand outpaces supply
- Stop taking "anything and everything" in panic mode

5. Numbers: Does the Math Math?

Finally, we put real numbers into the model.

For example:

If your target is **$1M in revenue**, and your **average client value is $5,000**, you need:

- 200 matters a year

- ~17 new matters per month

Can your team and systems handle that?

If not, you either:

- Increase your average client value
- Reduce scope and volume
- Add staff with a clear role and capacity model

Million-dollar firms aren't built on vibes.

They're built on math + mindset.

Marcus's Shift: From "Anything" to Aligned

Here's how Marcus reworked his model over 18–24 months:

1. **Simplified Case Types**
   - Focused on mid-to-high value criminal defense and contested divorces
   - Referred out or declined low-fee, high-drama work
   - Created a small referral circle for those "not our model" cases (and got referrals back for his focus areas)
2. **Restructured Fees**
   - Implemented tiered flat fees for specific phases
   - Set minimum fees that made sense for his life and firm
   - Stopped discounting in the room just because someone hesitated
3. **Redesigned Delivery**

- Paralegals handled routine filings, discovery requests, and client updates
- Junior attorneys took certain hearings under clear supervision
- He reserved his time for strategy, high-impact advocacy, and CEO duties

4. **Defined Capacity**

- Set a max active case count per attorney
- Used that to decide when to hire, when to raise prices, and when to pause intake in certain categories

Result?

- Fewer open matters
- Higher average revenue per case
- Less chaos
- More predictable cash flow
- Less of that "I'm drowning" feeling

Same man.

Different model.

Completely different life.

The First-Class Scorecard: Decide Like a CEO

To keep your business model honest, you need a simple **scorecard**.

Not 40 metrics.

Just a handful you look at weekly or monthly:

- **Revenue this month**
- **New matters opened**
- **Average client value**
- **Owner compensation paid**
- **True profit (Dessert)**
- **Cash in your Carbs (tax) account**
- **Open case count per attorney**

Those numbers tell the truth:

- If ACV is low and cases are high → too much meat, not enough quality
- If owner comp is low → your Vegetables are starving
- If profit is nonexistent → plate is out of balance
- If the case count is insane → your capacity and model are off

The goal is not perfection.

It's awareness.

Because when you can see what's happening, you can make **million-dollar decisions** instead of **midnight guesses**.

Your First-Class Action Step: Model Check

Before you move on, take 15–20 minutes and answer these questions honestly:

1. **What are the top 2–3 types of cases or matters that bring in the best money with the least chaos?**
2. **What are 2–3 types of cases you secretly hate but keep saying yes to?**

3. **Does your current pricing and capacity make it realistically possible to:**

    - Pay yourself well (Vegetables)
    - Set aside profit (Dessert)
    - Cover taxes without panic (Carbs)

If not, your model needs an upgrade—not more hustle.

Because a First-Class Firm isn't built on saying yes to everything.

It's built on a billion little decisions that all point in one direction:

A business that works, a team that supports it, and a life where you actually get to enjoy the dessert you designed this whole thing around.

CHAPTER 11

Seats, Not Saviors: Building a Firm That Doesn't Need You to Be the Hero

Let's be real:

Right now, if you disappeared for 60 days with no Wi-Fi, would your firm:

A) Keep running smoothly

B) Wobble but survive

C) Catch fire, fall apart, and text you every five minutes

If the answer is anywhere near C… you don't have an organization.

You have a group project where you're doing most of the work.

A First-Class Firm is not built on heroic effort.

It's built on **structure**.

The structure isn't stiff. It's supportive.

It takes the weight off your back and spreads it across systems, roles, and people.

This chapter is all about that structure—specifically, your **organizational chart** and how you think about **seats vs. people**.

Because until you get this right, you will keep "fixing" problems by throwing yourself at them.

Why Your Current "Structure" Is Exhausting You

Most small and mid-sized law firms are organized like this:

- The owner does everything important
- A few key people do a little bit of everything else
- Titles are vague: "assistant," "case manager," "helps with stuff."
- Every problem eventually rolls uphill… to you

On paper, you might have roles.

In real life, you have **vibes**.

You know it's bad when:

- The staff says, "Just ask [the owner], they'll know."
- Nobody is truly responsible for anything—just "we" and "they."
- You're CC'd on every email "just in case."
- Vacations feel like a dangerous luxury.

This is how you end up being:

- The rainmaker
- The lead attorney
- The HR department
- The head of marketing

- The therapist your staff vents to

…while wondering why you're so tired.

Seats vs. People: The First-Class Shift

Here's the mindset shift:

First-Class Firms are built around **seats**, not around **saviors**.

A **seat** is a role with clear responsibilities and outcomes.

A **savior** is "that one person who holds everything together."

You can love your team AND still design your firm around seats, not personalities.

Why this matters:

- People will eventually leave, change roles, or need time off
- Your future growth cannot depend on one "unicorn" staying forever
- Your brain needs to know: who owns what, and what success looks like.

Seats create **clarity**.

Clarity reduces **anxiety**.

Anxiety reduction is a business strategy.

The Three Levels of a First-Class Firm

No matter how big or small your firm is, a solid org chart usually has three major layers:

1. **Leadership** – Vision, decisions, direction

2. **Revenue & Delivery** – Lawyers and legal support who produce results
3. **Operations & Support** – The backbone that keeps everything moving

Let's break it down with an example.

We'll go back to **Legacy Path Estate Law** with Erica—now several years into her growth, headed toward and beyond the million-dollar mark.

Legacy Path 1.0: Everyone Does Everything

When Erica started, her "org chart" looked like this:

- Erica: Owner, lead attorney, closer, drafter, HR, financial decision-maker, marketing department
- Assistant: Phones, scheduling, random admin, light intake
- Contract drafter: Documents "when needed"

There were only three humans, but ten jobs—and Erica had eight of them.

The result:

- Every decision flowed through her
- Nobody was sure who was really "in charge" of what
- When Erica had a bad day, the whole firm had a bad week

That's fine at $150K.

It's unsustainable at $750K.

It's a breakdown waiting to happen at $1M+.

Legacy Path 2.0: Designing the Seats

We started by ignoring *who* was currently there and asking:

"If this were a million-plus First-Class Firm, with sane hours and strong profit… what seats would exist?"

We mapped out seats like this:

Leadership Layer

- CEO / Managing Attorney (owner)
- Operations Manager (eventually)

Revenue & Delivery Layer

- Lead Estate Planning Attorney
- Associate Attorney(s)
- Senior Paralegal (estate planning)
- Junior Paralegal / Legal Assistant

Operations & Support Layer

- Intake & Client Experience Coordinator
- Administrative Assistant / Office Coordinator
- Bookkeeper / outsourced CFO support
- Marketing Coordinator (part-time or contractor)

At first, Erica said, "That's too many people. I can't afford that."

Misconception.

We weren't saying, "Hire everybody tomorrow."

We were saying, "Design the **structure** first, then grow into it intentionally."

Even with only a few team members, you can:

- Assign multiple **seats** to one person
- Separate **responsibilities** on paper
- See where future hires would go

That alone calms your brain. You can see the **plan**, not just the chaos.

Every Seat Needs a Win

For each seat, we defined:

- **Primary purpose** – Why does this seat exist?
- **Top 3–5 responsibilities** – What must this seat own?
- **Success metrics** – How do we know they're doing well?

For example, the **Intake & Client Experience Coordinator** seat:

- **Purpose:** Convert qualified leads into signed clients and provide a smooth pre-engagement experience.
- **Responsibilities:**
  - Answer and return calls quickly
  - Qualify leads using clear criteria
  - Schedule and confirm consults
  - Follow up with undecided prospects
- **Success Metrics:**
  - Number of consults booked per week

- Show-up rate
- Conversion rate from consult to signed client

Now, instead of "my assistant helps with intake," We have a **seat** with clear wins.

Clarity like that makes:

- Training easier
- Feedback less emotional
- Accountability possible

It also helps your nervous system calm down because you're no longer managing vibes—you're managing outcomes.

Boundary Work, But Make It Organizational

Here's where mindset sneaks in again.

When we defined seats, Erica struggled with:

- Letting go of tasks ("I feel bad dumping this on them")
- Expecting performance ("I don't want to be too hard on people")
- Saying no when people blur the lines ("Can you just handle this one thing…")

That's not just management discomfort.

That's old survival programming:

- "Don't be too demanding."
- "Don't upset people who are helping you."
- "I'd rather hurt myself than confront somebody."

But an unclear org chart is just **blurred boundaries** at the business level.

You're not just protecting your time with this structure. You're protecting your **mental health**.

Because when everybody knows:

- What they're responsible for
- Where their authority starts and ends
- Who do they go to with what

Your days stop feeling like you're playing whack-a-mole with grown adults.

Scaling Without Losing Your Mind

As Legacy Path grew, the org chart helped Erica make **calm decisions**:

- When the intake volume increased, and consults were booked out?
- → Time to add capacity in the Intake seat.
- When drafting, was the turnaround lagging?
- → Evaluate the Paralegal seat first, not jump in and "save the day."
- When Erica's time as CEO kept getting eaten by random tasks?
- → Ask: "Is there a seat for this? If not, do we need one?"

Instead of reacting, she could **diagnose**.

The org chart became:

- A planning tool
- A hiring roadmap
- A reality check

It also made it easier to say:

"You're doing great in these seats. This one either needs more support or needs to move to someone else."

Adult conversations. With data. Less drama.

You Are Not a Department

Here's a question I want you to sit with:

"Which departments am I pretending to be, all by myself?"

Be honest. Right now, you might be:

- Legal department
- Marketing department
- Finance department
- HR department
- Operations department

No wonder you're tired.

A First-Class Firm doesn't mean you never wear multiple hats—especially early on.

But it does mean:

- You're aware of which hats you're wearing
- You're making a plan to hand them off over time

- You're not letting guilt or fear keep you stuck in every seat forever

We're not glorifying grinds here.

We're designing a business that lets you climb without collapsing.

Your First-Class Action Step: Draft Your "Seats-First" Org Chart

Before you move on, I want you to do this—yes, actually do it:

1. **List the three layers for YOUR firm:**
    - Leadership
    - Revenue & Delivery
    - Operations & Support
2. Under each, write down the **ideal seats** you would have if your firm were running at $1M+ with sanity and strong profit.
3. Then, next to each seat, write:
    - Who currently sits there (you, a team member, nobody yet)
    - Whether that seat is clear, fuzzy, or non-existent

This becomes:

- Your hiring roadmap
- Your delegation plan
- Your reality check when you feel overwhelmed

Because the goal isn't just to build a bigger firm.

It's to build a **structured**, First-Class Firm where:

- You are well-compensated
- Your team knows what they're doing
- The business can function even when you're not in the building

No more savior.

No more hero syndrome.

Just a clear, well-fed CEO sitting in the seat only they can fill—and a firm that finally has the structure to match the vision.

CHAPTER 12

First-Class or Nothing: Designing a Life You Don't Need a Vacation From

Let's end this book the same way we started it:

With dessert on the table.

Because if your firm grows, but **you** are still exhausted, underpaid, anxious, and one late payment away from spiraling, then we did not build a First-Class Firm.

We just built a more expensive version of survival.

And let me be clear: survival may have been necessary in one season of your life, but it is not supposed to be your permanent business model.

This book was never just about making more money.

It was about making your money, your mindset, your team, your systems, and your business model line up with the life you actually want.

A life where:

- your firm generates real revenue,
- your profit is intentional,

- your compensation reflects your value,
- your team is not draining the life out of you,
- your systems don't fall apart when you step away,
- and your success doesn't come at the expense of your peace.

That is what I call a **First-Class Firm**.

And if you've made it this far, I need you to hear me:

You are too smart, too gifted, and too far along in your journey to keep building a business that makes everybody else comfortable while you stay stressed.

That season has to end.

First-Class Is Bigger Than Revenue

Yes, we've talked about the numbers throughout this book:

- **$1M+ in revenue**
- **$100K+ in profit**
- **$100K+ in owner's compensation**

Those are powerful benchmarks.

But a First-Class Firm is not just defined by the numbers in your accounting software. It is also defined by the quality of the life attached to those numbers.

A First-Class Firm means:

- You're not dodging your CPA's emails because you're scared of what the tax bill will be.
- You can pay your team **and** pay yourself.

- You can take a vacation without acting like your laptop is your emotional support animal.
- You can look at your bank account without your chest tightening up.
- You can make strategic decisions from a place of clarity instead of panic.
- You can actually enjoy the business you worked so hard to build.

Because let's be honest: too many law firm owners have built businesses that look successful from the outside but feel exhausting on the inside.

They have the revenue.

They have the clients.

They have the nice branding.

But they do not have peace.

And I don't know about you, but I'm not interested in helping people build pretty prisons.

You Cannot Take Poverty Rules Into a First-Class Life

If there is one theme that runs through this entire book, it is this:

You cannot take poverty rules into a First-Class life.

You cannot keep saying:

- "I'll pay myself after everybody else is good."
- "I don't want to charge too much."

- "I'll just take one more case, even though I know it's going to be a headache."
- "I don't want to hold my team accountable because I don't want to seem mean."
- "I'll rest later."
- "I should just be grateful."

No.

That kind of thinking may have helped you survive in another chapter of your life, but it will sabotage you in this one.

A First-Class Firm requires a First-Class mindset.

That means you have to become the kind of person who believes:

- it is safe to make money,
- it is safe to keep money,
- it is safe to be visible,
- it is safe to say no,
- it is safe to lead,
- and it is safe to build a business that serves your life instead of stealing it.

That is not arrogance.

That is alignment.

The Real Goal

Let's make sure we are crystal clear on the real goal.

The goal is not just to say, "My firm made a million dollars."

The goal is to be able to say:

- "My firm made a million dollars, and I'm not burned out."
- "My firm made a million dollars, and I'm compensated well."
- "My firm made a million dollars, and I have systems that work."
- "My firm made a million dollars, and my team is aligned."
- "My firm made a million dollars, and I still have a life."

That is the difference between a firm that simply grows and a firm that is truly **First-Class**.

Because a lot of people can hit a big revenue year by accident, adrenaline, or sheer force.

But sustaining that kind of business with:

- profit,
- structure,
- peace,
- and mental health intact?

That takes intention.

That takes leadership.

That takes a different level of support.

You Do Not Need More Information. You Need Implementation.

By now, you've read the concepts.

You've seen the framework.

You understand the food groups:

- **Dessert** for profit
- **Carbs** for tax savings
- **Vegetables** for owner benefits
- **Meat** for operating expenses

You've learned about:

- hiring,
- leadership,
- systems,
- technology,
- marketing,
- pricing,
- networking,
- business modeling,
- and structure.

So at this point, your problem is probably not lack of information.

Your problem is likely one of three things:

1. You know what needs to happen, but you have not made the time to implement it.
2. You know what needs to happen, but you need support, accountability, and strategy to execute it correctly.

3. You know what needs to happen, but your mindset, fear, or past money story keeps pulling you back into the same patterns.

And that is exactly why I do the work I do.

Because information alone does not change your life.

Implementation does.

Support does.

Strategy does.

Having somebody who can look at your firm objectively, tell you the truth, and help you build a plan that actually fits your goals does.

You Don't Have to Figure This Out Alone

Let me keep it real with you:

You can absolutely take what you've learned in this book and start making changes on your own.

And I hope you do.

But if you are reading this and thinking:

- "I'm tired of guessing."
- "I know I'm leaving money on the table."
- "I know my systems are messy."
- "I know I'm underpaid."
- "I know my firm has more potential than what I'm currently experiencing."

- "I need help getting from where I am to a true First-Class Firm."

Then I want you to stop overthinking it.

This is your sign to get support.

You do not need another year of:

- overworking,
- underpaying yourself,
- carrying your whole firm on your back,
- and calling it "just part of entrepreneurship."

No.

At some point, growth requires a different level of guidance.

And if you are serious about elevating your life, your firm, and your finances, then the next step is simple.

Your Next Step

If you are ready to create a **First-Class Firm**—one that is profitable, structured, scalable, and designed to support the life you actually want—I want you to schedule a call with me.

Go to:

talktojayden.com

That's it.

Go to **talktojayden.com** and schedule a call so we can talk about:

- where your firm is right now,

- what's keeping you stuck,
- what needs to shift,
- and how I can help you build a First-Class Firm that actually works for your life.

Not a cute theory.

Not a motivational moment.

Not another notebook full of ideas you never implement.

A real plan.

Real strategy.

Real elevation.

Because if you've connected with what I've shared in this book, then you already know I'm not here to play with your potential.

I'm here to help you build something that pays you, protects you, and positions you for the next level.

Final Boarding Call

You've read the book.

You've got the framework.

You know the truth now.

So the question is not whether you are capable.

The question is whether you are ready to stop settling for a business that looks successful but feels heavy.

Are you ready to:

- stop being the last one paid,

- stop making emotional money decisions,
- stop undercharging,
- stop operating without structure,
- stop hiding,
- and stop building a firm that runs you instead of the other way around?

If the answer is yes, then do not just close this book, nod your head, and go back to business as usual.

Take action.

Go to **talktojayden.com** and schedule your call.

Let's talk about what it would look like for you to create a First-Class Firm.

Not someday.

Now.

Because you did not come this far to keep flying coach in your business, your finances, or your life.

It is time to elevate.

And when you are ready, I'll be ready.

Meet me at **talktojayden.com**.

About The Author

Jayden Doyé, also known as Thee Law Firm's CPA, has taken the CPA industry by storm, bringing his charismatic personality with him. But, he was not always the financial guru that he is today. Growing up in a household, just shy of the federal poverty line in Prince George's County, MD although not being raised with the tools to create financial growth, he understood the benefits of economic stability. He was on a mission to achieve it. His journey began at Towson University where a B.S. in Accounting was completed along with a large amount of student debt. Having learned to confront challenges head-on, Jayden saw this as an opportunity to grow rather than a setback.

Transferring this same tenacity and A LOT of sacrifice to his career, Jayden gained professional experience as an accountant at a small CPA firm in Atlanta and became a Certified Public Accountant. Driven by a relentless pursuit of knowledge and a passion for financial acumen, he attained his CPA designation and refined his expertise in legal accounting. For more than 10 years he's worked with clients in several industries - helping them expand their financial portfolios, and create plans that ensure economic sustainability, and minimize taxability.

During the first two years of building his own CPA firm, Prestige Accounting Solutions, Jayden, as president discovered his niche- law firm owners. He realized that many desire his lifestyle living debt-free, a monthly mandatory vacation, and delegating/elevating a team to operate a profitable business that does not require the owner's full attention. Prestige Accounting Solutions specializes in empowering law firms to optimize their profitability. In business, Jayden became a Certified Profit First Professional; now he teaches the Profit First method to business owners which guarantees that their business generates profits.

Jayden Doyé is a bestselling author and internationally acclaimed speaker. He is renowned for his training, which is deeply insightful and thought-provoking. His topics range from business development, client acquisition, hiring profitably, and utilizing technology. He has held numerous workshops globally on the value of connection, understanding, and collaboration in growing a business. He became a best-selling author in 2022 by Amazon, a distinction that speaks to his influence and impact as an author. With an extraordinary ability to connect with people on a profound level and an incomparable capacity to captivate audiences with his words and thoughts, Jayden Doyé's work has touched thousands of lives across the globe. Jayden is also a member of several professional organizations including the American Institute of Certified Professional Accountants, the National Association of Certified Bookkeepers and The Georgia Society of CPA's.

As a CPA, Jayden Doyé's goal is to help entrepreneurs like himself, gain independence, eliminate debt, and create unique action plans to bring more to their bottom line while paying less taxes. His professional journey has been shaped by a deep commitment to financial excellence and a steadfast dedication to helping others succeed. Invest in yourself and start working with Jayden TODAY!

talktojayden.com

Made in the USA
Coppell, TX
12 June 2026

81280509R10085